JESUS, LORD

JESUS
LORD

SELECTED PASSAGES ON OUR LORD FROM THE
WRITINGS OF THE
FATHERS, DOCTORS AND THEOLOGIANS
FROM THE "FATHERS OF THE CHURCH" SERIES,
PUBLISHED BY
THE CATHOLIC UNIVERSITY OF AMERICA PRESS.

COMPILED BY

FATHER CHARLES DOLLEN

**Library Director
University of San Diego**

ST. PAUL EDITIONS

86727

BR
63
D6

Library of Congress Catalog Card Number: 64-17753

FOR

CHARLES EUGENE HUNT

CONTENTS

1. *In the beginning was the Word* 19

ST. AMBROSE:
The Sacrament of the Incarnation of the Lord 21

ST. JOHN CHRYSOSTOM:
Homilies on St. John 25

ST. AUGUSTINE:
The City of God 29

ST. LEO THE GREAT
Letter to Flavian 33

ST. AUGUSTINE
Confessions 39

EUSEBIUS:
Ecclesiastical History 43

2. *Emmanuel!* 48

ST. JUSTIN, MARTYR:
The First Apology 50

ST. LEO THE GREAT:
The Testimony 53

ST. PETER CHRYSOLOGUS:
The Annunciation 59

ST. JUSTIN, MARTYR:
Dialogue with Trypho 63

ST. JOHN DAMASCENE:
The Orthodox Faith 68

ST. BERNARD:
On the Canticle of Canticles 74

PRUDENTIUS:
Hymns 77

3. *The Son of Man* 79

EUSEBIUS:
Ecclesiastical History 81

ST. IGNATIUS OF ANTIOCH:
Letters 85

ST. LEO THE GREAT:
Letter to Emperor Leo 88

ST. BASIL:
Letters 94

ST. JOHN DAMASCENE:
The Orthodox Faith 97

ST. BERNARD:
On the Circumcision 103

4. *The wondrous works of God* 106

CLEMENT OF ALEXANDRIA:
Christ the Educator 108

ST. AMBROSE:
Second Oration on Faith in the Resurrection 114

ST. BASIL:
Letters 119

12

ST. CYPRIAN:
   The Good of Patience 124
ST. VALERIAN:
   On Mercy 129
ST. BASIL:
   Homily on Psalm 33 134
ST. AUGUSTINE:
   Sermon on the Mount 138
ST. NICETA OF REMESIANA:
   The Names and Titles of Our Savior 145
PRUDENTIUS:
   Hymns 149

5. The Kingdom of God 152

ST. AMBROSE:
   The Mysteries 154
ST. BASIL:
   Homily on Psalm 28 158
ST. BASIL:
   Concerning Baptism 161
TERTULLIAN:
   On Prayer 168
ST. CAESARIUS OF ARLES:
   On the Lord's Prayer 172
ST. CYPRIAN:
   The Unity of the Church 177
ST. JOHN CHRYSOSTOM:
   Homilies on John 180
ST. BASIL:
   Homily on Psalm 44 184

ST. CLEMENT OF ROME:
Letter to the Corinthians 188

6. *Man of Sorrows* 193

ST. JOHN CHRYSOSTOM:
Homilies on St. John 195

ST. AMBROSE:
Letters to Priests 202

ST. AMBROSE:
The Holy Spirit 205

ST. AMBROSE:
Letters to Bishops 208

TERTULLIAN:
The Apology 211

ST. HILARY OF POITIERS:
The Trinity 215

ST. AUGUSTINE:
Against Julian 222

PRUDENTIUS:
Hymns 226

7. *Alleluia!* 229

ST. AUGUSTINE:
The City of God 231

ST. PETER CHRYSOLOGUS:
Christ's Resurrection 236

ST. CLEMENT OF ROME:
Second Letter to the Corinthians 242

ST. AUGUSTINE:
Faith and Works 245

ST. GREGORY THE GREAT:
Dialogues 250

ST. AUGUSTINE:
The Creed 254

ST. AMBROSE:
Letters to Laymen 258

ST. AUGUSTINE:
On the Trinity 264

LIVING VOICES—A POSTSCRIPT 271

MEET THE AUTHORS 273

WITNESS OF THE AGES 277

INDEX 279

15

JESUS, LORD

"And no one can say 'Jesus is Lord' except in the Holy Spirit."
(1 Cor. 12:3) Trust St. Paul to go right to the heart of matters
and to be willing to stand up and be counted. When it came to
recognizing and accepting the divinity of Christ, he embraced
the doctrine whole-heartedly. It became the guiding light of all
his theology. But he understood that faith in the God-man was a
great grace, freely given by a magnificent Father.

Further, he saw that faith could be a sterile intellectual exercise,
or a living, vital spiritual gift. The first he rejected; the second
he proclaimed. And this living faith he placed as the first of the
spiritual gifts given by the Holy Spirit. To live all that is implied
in the phrase "Jesus is Lord" means living a perfect Christian
life, guided by faith, surging forward in hope, burning with
charity, a supple instrument in the designs of the Holy Spirit.
Quite simply, it means becoming a saint.

In the passages which follow, we have ample testimony to the
living faith of the early Christian Church in the divinity of
Christ and what this implied in the lives of the everyday Christian. The Fathers of the Church delved deeply into the Scriptures

16

and brought out treasures both old and new. They knew that their loving heavenly Father was the Jahweh of old; they knew that the word Adonai was transposed in reading the Scriptures to preserve the name of God. Therefore, when Christ was called "Lord" (Adonai), they proclaimed his equality with God.

And they never hesitated to acknowledge the Lordship, the divinity, of Jesus Christ. When they taught the faithful to live Christian lives, it was because Christ was God. When they urged, cajoled or corrected, in season or out of season, it was because Jesus Christ was the God-made-man, the Model, par excellence, the motivation. When they jousted with heretics it was to exult in the glories of Christ, God-Incarnate. "Jesus is Lord" means "I believe that Jesus Christ is the Son of God and the Son of Man, true God and true man; and, I am following Him." Certainly, it must be said "in the Holy Spirit."

* * * *

The excerpts that follow are from the FATHERS OF THE CHURCH series, published by the Catholic University of America press. Dr. Roy Joseph Deferrari is the general editor of the series, heading a distinguished editorial board. The translators of the volumes so far published have done a thorough and skillful job, one that is also, obviously, a labor of love. It is a tribute to American Catholic scholarship that this series can be produced. Rather than append a bibliography to this volume, it is hoped that these excerpts will serve as an invitation to the reader to drink more deeply from the well of patristic literature so ably presented in THE FATHERS OF THE CHURCH.

The two passages from St. Bernard are free translations of the editor of this book, who can never pass over the inspiring texts of "the last of the Fathers." A word of thanks must also be said to the Rev. Dr. Joseph Egan, who made patrology an adventure for a whole generation of seminarians.

17

Chapter 1

IN
THE
BEGINNING
WAS
THE
WORD

In the beginning was the Word,
and the Word was with God,
and the Word was God.

St. John 1:1

With what simple words St. John begins the story of the eternal love of God! We would expect Cherubim and Seraphim to explode in canticles of praise and joy while angels and archangels trumpeted the news through the ages. Yet the mystery of the Holy Trinity, with the intensity of love that is its inner life and the sublime activity that is a divine romance, is revealed to us in humble language.

For the Son of God is the perfect image of the invisible God, His Father. He is the understanding and expression of the Father's knowledge of Himself. This awareness of His total divinity the Father expresses in a Word—His co-equal, co-eternal, consubstantial Son, "begotten not made, God of God, light of light." And the Son returns this awareness of divinity in the Father and from them the Holy Spirit proceeds, the personal bond of Love, co-equal, co-eternal, consubstantial.

St. John was so caught up in his love for Christ that he could only seek to penetrate the mystery of his Lord as deeply and as perfectly as reason and revelation would allow. Therefore, he begins his Christ-centered spirituality with "In the beginning was the Word." Nothing else would do for him, and he passes on the challenge to us.

Our lives, too, must be Christ-centered. Our every action must be guided by the question, "What does Christ want?" We search through the Scriptures, the teachings of the Church, and the lessons of history to find out what Christ did and what He said. In the search, and in searching, we must constantly co-operate with God's grace in the formation of Christ in our souls.

It is in this spirit that the great religious movements of our day take on meaning. The ecumenical movement in its great desire for Christian unity will be lasting and effective only if it is Christ-centered. No matter what the effort or the sacrifice, unity can be achieved only in Christ, only when all seek the will of Christ, in spirit and truth. Pope Paul VI understands this, as his pilgrimage to the Holy Land demonstrated so clearly.

The liturgical renewal initiated by the Second Vatican Council is another dramatically valid effort to emphasize the Christocentric character of our life in God. How else can a man make any progress spiritually? Even the noble desire to extend the Kingdom of God is meaningless unless it revolves around Christ, the Son of God, the Word made flesh.

And so, we must start at the beginning, and "In the beginning was the Word . . .".

ST. AMBROSE:

The Sacrament of the Incarnation of the Lord

I do not wish that credence be given us; let the Scripture be quoted. Not of myself do I say: "In the beginning was the Word," but I hear it. Who says this? Surely, John the fisherman, but he does not say this as a fisherman, but as a fisher of man's disposition. For already he was not catching fish but was quickening men.

These words are not his, but His who granted him the power of quickening. For the fisherman was more silent than the fish which he formerly used to catch, and with respect to the divine mysteries, he was more dumb who did not know the author of his own voice; but he who is quickened by Christ has heard the voice in John, has recognized the Word in Christ.

Accordingly, full of the Holy Spirit, since he knew that the beginning was not of time, but above time, he left the world, and ascending in spirit above all beginning, he says, "In the beginning was the Word," that is, let the heavens remain, for they were not yet, since "in the beginning was the Word." For, although the heavens have a beginning, God does not have one.

Excerpts from Chapters 3, 5, and 9

Finally, "In the beginning God made heaven and earth." "Made" is one thing; "was" another. What is made has a beginning; what was, does not receive a beginning, but comes before. Let time also remain, because time is after the heavens. Let also the angels and the archangels remain. And if I do not discover their beginning, yet there was a time when they were not. For they were not who at some time began. If, then, I cannot discover the beginning of those who certainly had a beginning, how can I discover the beginning of the Word, from whom all beginning, not only of creatures, but also of all our thoughts springs.

Thus had John clearly declared the everlasting divinity of the Word, but yet, lest anyone might separate the eternity of the Word from the Father, that we might believe that it is the same for the Word as for the Father, the good fisherman added: "And the Word was God." What he said is to be understood thus: "The Word was just as was the Father; since He was together with the Father, He was also in the Father, and He was always with the Father."

It is of the Word to be with the Father; it is of the Father to be with the Word, for we read that "the Word was with God." Lest perchance you slip in the use of human speech, when you say "Word" and "Son," he accordingly added: "And the Word was God."

Surely He has what the Father has, because He was God. How do you deny the eternity of Him who together with the Father has the one name of God? Let not the sound and the similarity of the expression deceive you. The word which is temporal, which is put together with syllables and is composed of letters, is one thing; the Son is not such a Word, because the Father of the Word is not such.

"What we have seen and what we have heard," says St. John. This only he related, which he knew well, what he heard and what he saw, he who leaned on the bosom of Christ. But what he heard, this he tells, and what he has heard from Christ, this I cannot deny is the truth about Christ. For he saw what he saw, certainly not divinity, which cannot be seen according to its nature.

But, because He could not be seen according to His nature, He took on what was outside the nature of divinity, that He might be seen according to the nature of body. The day will fail me sooner than the names of heretics and different sects, yet against all is this general faith–that Christ is the Son of God, and eternal from the Father, and born of the Virgin Mary.

What, now, is so much of one nature as our flesh with the true body of the Lord? Yet they have both been brought forth by different causes, have arisen from different beginnings. For the flesh of the Lord, generated when the Spirit came to the Virgin, did not await the customary intercourse of male and female union; but our flesh, unless the male and female sex bring genital seed to the natural channels, cannot be formed within the maternal womb; and yet, although the cause of generation was different, nevertheless the flesh of Christ is of one nature with all men.

For childbirth did not change the nature of the Virgin, but established a new method of generating. So flesh was born of flesh. Thus the Virgin had of her own what she gave; for the mother did not give something of another, but she contributed her own from her womb in an unusual manner, but in a usual function.

Therefore, the Virgin had the flesh, which by customary right of nature she transferred to the fetus. Therefore the nature of Mary, who gave birth, and that of the Begotten are the same according to the flesh, and not unlike His human brethren, because Scripture says: "In all things to be made like to His brethren." Surely the Son of God is like to us not according to the fullness of divinity, but according to our rational soul, and, to speak more clearly, according to the truth of our human body.

ST. JOHN CHRYSOSTOM:

Homilies on St. John

Come then, let us once more bring our discussion to the opening words: "In the beginning was the Word, and the Word was with God." Why is it that, while all the other evangelists begin from the Incarnation, John merely hints briefly at the Incarnation by saying further on: "And the Word was made flesh." Why does he omit all the other details—His conception, His birth, upbringing, growth—and talk to us about His eternal generation? What the reason for this is I shall tell you now.

Since the other evangelists had spent much time in outlining the details which pertain to His humanity, there would be cause to fear lest some earthly-minded individuals might, in consequence, remain content with these teachings only. It was, then, to draw up from this striving after things of the earth those who were likely to relapse into it, and to direct them upward to heaven, that he deliberately made the introduction of his narrative open from on high and from the eternal existence.

While Matthew entered upon his narrative from King Herod, Luke from Tiberius Caesar, and Mark from the baptism of John, he omitted all these

Excerpts from the fourth homily

details, mounted higher than all time and ages, and precipitated the understanding of his listeners on the words: "In the beginning." And he did not allow it to halt in any place, or set any limitation on it, as they did in Herod, and Tiberius, and John.

Besides this, what may be mentioned as especially admirable is that he who began his discourse on a higher plane has not neglected the Incarnation, nor have the other evangelists who hastened to begin their narrative with this subject been silent about the eternal existence; and very reasonably so. It was one Spirit who inspired the souls of all four, and therefore they showed great unanimity in their narratives.

And, beloved, when you hear "Word," do not consent to the opinion of those who declare that the Word Itself is a work of the Creator or the opinion that It is simply a word. Many, to be sure, are the words of God, which even angels carry out, but no one of them is God.

This Word, however, is a Being, a distinct Person, proceeding from the Father Himself without alteration. He has indicated this by his appellation "the Word." Therefore just as the expression "In the beginning was the Word" reveals His eternity, so "He was in the beginning with God" has revealed to us His co-eternity. Lest on hearing: "In the beginning was the Word," you might think that He was indeed eternal, but suppose that the life of the Father was older by some interval of time, and might consequently concede that the Only-begotten had a beginning, he has added the sentence: "He was in the beginning with God." That is, He was as eternal as the Father Himself, for the Father was never without the Word, but always God was with God, though each in His own Person.

Once he had said "And the Word was God," in order that no one might think that the Godhead of the Son was inferior, he at once predicated of Him characteristics recognized as marks of genuine divinity, both referring again to His eternity, by declaring: "He was in the beginning with God," and mentioning also His power of creating, for: "All things were made by Him, and without Him was made nothing that has been made."

This latter power, in particular, His Father frequently declares by the prophets, is a characteristic mark of His own essence. Indeed, the prophets repeatedly use this point in support of the Godhead, and not merely for its own sake, but also in their struggle against the honor given idols. One says: "The gods that have not made heaven and earth, let them perish." And another: "I stretch out the heavens by my hand." And everywhere that this point is set down, it is to show that it is indicative of the Godhead.

Therefore, let us glorify Him as we have learned from our fathers. Let us glorify Him by our faith and our works. Pious teachings avail us nothing for salvation if our life has become corrupted. Therefore, let us order it according to the will of God. In this way we shall truly overcome and win the rewards: both those granted here and those promised to us by the grace and mercy of Our Lord Jesus Christ, through whom glory, power and honor be to the Father, together with the Holy Spirit, now and always, and forever and ever. Amen.

ST. AUGUSTINE:

The City of God

But, if it be inevitable that all men, so long as they are mortal, must also be miserable—a contention far more credible and probable—then we must seek a mediator who is not only human, but also divine, in order that, by the intervention of His blessed mortality, men may be led from their mortal misery to a blessed immortality. It was necessary for this mediator to become, but not to remain, mortal.

Indeed, He became incarnate not by any diminution of the divinity of the Word, but by assuming the frailty of flesh. This flesh He raised from the dead, but He did not remain mortal in the flesh. The very fruit of His mediation is precisely this: that they for whose liberation He became a mediator should not remain forever subject even to the death of the flesh.

Thus the mediator between men and God was to possess a passing mortality and an enduring beatitude, so that, by means of a passing element, He might be conformed to men who are mortal and then transport them from death to that which endures. Therefore, the good angels cannot be mediators between miserable mortals and happy immortals, be-

Excerpts from Book 9

cause they, also, are both blessed and immortal. The wicked angels could, because they are immortal like the blessed and unhappy like men.

But, ranged against these is the good mediator, who, to oppose their immortality and misery, was willing to become mortal for a time though able to remain blessed for eternity. Thus, lest those proud immortals and miserable mischief-makers, by boasting of their immortality, should seduce men to misery, He, by the humility of His death and the benignity of His beatitude has destroyed their diabolic reign in those whose hearts He cleansed by faith and liberation from their unclean dominion.

What kind of mediator then, should miserable and mortal man, far removed from the blessed immortals, choose in order to reach a blessed immortality? All that could please him in the immortality of demons is misery and nothing that might offend him in the mortality of Christ any longer exists. We must beware, therefore, of eternal misery with demons, whereas with Christ, death is not even to be feared, since it could not last forever, and happiness can be loved everlastingly.

Whenever the devil, the immortal and miserable mediator, intervenes, it is to prevent men from attaining blessed immortality, since the demon's misery that prevents this for himself is unending. But the reason why a mortal and blessed mediator intervened was in order that, having lived through His mortality, He might give to those subject to death, immortality—as He has shown by His resurrection—and, to the miserable, beatitude, which He Himself never lost.

Therefore, the evil mediator who separates friends is altogether different from the good one who reconciles enemies. Now, the reason for the multitude of mediators who separate lies is the multitude of those who are blessed—and beatified by their participation in one God. It is the privation of this participation that makes the miserable multitude of evil angels oppose us as an impediment, rather than interpose as an aid in the attaining of this beatitude. And their multiplicity, too, in a certain sense, is an obstacle in the way of our reaching that one Supreme Beatitude, to reach which we needed not many but one mediator—*the* Mediator, in communion with whom alone we can be blessed, namely, the uncreated Word of God, by whom all things were created.

However, the fact that He is the Word is not the reason why He is the mediator; for certainly, the Word at the summit of immortality and the apex of beatitude is far removed from miserable mortals. Rather He is the mediator because He is man, and as man shows us that to attain that supreme Good, blessed and beatific, we need not seek other mediators to serve like rungs on a ladder of ascent.

For, the blessed God who makes us blessed, by deigning to share our humanity, showed us the shortest way to sharing His divinity. Freeing us from mortality and misery, He leads us, not to the immortal blessed angels to become immortal and blessed by sharing in their nature, but to that Trinity in communion with which even the angels are blessed. When, then, in order to be Mediator, He willed to take the "nature of a slave" below the angels, He remained in the form of God above the angels, being at the same time the way of life on earth and life itself in heaven.

ST. LEO THE GREAT:

Letter to Flavian

But the birth of Our Lord, singularly wonderful and wonderfully singular, must not be understood as meaning that, because of the new type of procreation, the intrinsic quality of the birth was changed. Fecundity was given to the Virgin by the Holy Spirit, but the reality of the body was taken from her body; and with Wisdom building a dwelling for Himself, "The Word was made flesh and dwelt among us;" that is, in the flesh which He took from a human being and which He animated with the breath of rational life.

In this preservation, then, of the real quality of both natures, both being united in one person, lowliness was taken on by majesty, weakness by strength, mortality by the immortal. And in order to pay the debt of our fallen state, inviolable nature was united to one capable of suffering so that (and this is the sort of reparation we needed) one and the same Mediator between God and man, the man Jesus Christ, could die in one nature and not die in the other.

In the whole and perfect nature of the true man, then, the true God was born, complete in

Excerpts from Letter 28

His own nature, complete in ours. He took on the aspect of servitude without the stain of sin; He added to the humanity but did not lessen the divinity. He who, keeping the form of God, created man, the same was made man in the form of servitude.

The Son of God, then, enters into this weakness of the world, coming down from His heavenly throne, begotten in a new type of birth, but not departing from His Father's glory in the new order. The "order was new" in that, being invisible in His own nature, He became visible in ours; incomprehensible, He desired to be comprehended; enduring before time began, He began to exist in time. The Lord of the universe assumed the aspect of servitude with a shadow veiling the immensity of His majesty.

A God incapable of suffering, He deigned to become a man who could suffer, and being immortal, to become subject to the laws of death. He was born in a "new type of birth" in that undefiled virginity which experienced no concupiscence, yet supplied the material for the flesh. From the Mother the Lord took His nature, but no fault. The Lord Jesus Christ, born in a virgin's womb, does not have a different nature from ours just because His birth was an unusual one. He who is true God is also true man; there is no falsity in this union,

The Presentation of Jesus in the Temple (particular), GIOTTO
Chapel of the Scrovegni, Padua

"Being invisible in His own nature, He became visible in ours;
incomprehensible, He desired to be comprehended;
enduring before time began, He began to exist in time."

ST. LEO THE GREAT

wherein the lowliness of man and the greatness of divinity are mutually united.

Just as God is not changed by His show of mercy, so the man is not changed by being swallowed up in majesty. Each aspect performs its own acts in cooperation with the other; that is, the Word doing what is proper to the Word, the flesh pursuing what pertains to the flesh. The first of these is ablaze with the miraculous; the other is overpowered with injuries. And just as the Word does not give up any of His equality in the Father's glory, so also the flesh does not abandon the nature of our species. He is one and the same, truly Son of God and truly Son of man.

He is God because of the fact that "in the beginning was the Word and the Word was with God, and the Word was God"; and man through the fact that "the Word was made flesh and dwelt among us." He is God because "all things were made through Him, and without Him nothing was made;" a man through the fact that "He was born of a woman, born under the Law." The birth of flesh is a manifestation of human nature; that a virgin should give birth is a show of divine power.

The infancy of the babe is displayed by the lowliness of the cradle; the greatness of the Almighty is proclaimed by the voices of angels. He has a man's helpless infancy in that Herod impiously tries to kill Him; but He is the Lord of all, before whom the Magi kneel in supplication. Already, when He came to be baptized by John, the Precursor, lest it be unknown that divinity was being covered by a veil of flesh, the voice of the Father thundering from heaven said: "This is my beloved Son in whom I am well pleased."

To hunger, to thirst, to grow tired and to sleep: these are evidently human. But to satisfy 5,000 men with five loaves of bread and to give the Samaritan woman living water, a drink which frees the one drinking from further thirst, to walk on top of the sea without sinking and to calm the waves stirred up by a storm—are doubtless the work of God. Just as it is not part of the same nature to weep over a dead friend from the emotion of pity and then by command of His voice to call forth this man alive; or to hang on a cross of wood and yet to open the doors of paradise to the faithful thief—so also to say: "I and the Father are one," and to say: "The Father is greater than I," are not both pertinent to the same nature. From us He has a humanity less than the Father; from the Father a divinity equal to the Father's.

Because, then, of this union of personality (to be understood of both natures) the "Son of man," as we read, came down from heaven when the "Son of

God" assumed flesh from the Virgin through whom He was born. And again, the "Son of God" is said to have been crucified and buried, although this did not pertain to His divinity as such, in which the Only-begotten is co-eternal and consubstantial with the Father; but He endured this in the weakness of His human nature. Hence, too, we all profess in the Creed that the only-begotten "Son of God" was crucified and buried, according to the statement of the Apostle: "For had they known it, they never would have crucified the Lord of glory."

When Our Lord and Savior was teaching the faith to His disciples, He questioned them, saying: "Who do men say that I, the Son of Man, am?" And when they had given Him various opinions of others, He said: "But who do you say that I am?" That is, I, who am the Son of man and one whom you see in a condition of servitude and the reality of the flesh, whom do you say that I am?

When blessed Peter by divine inspiration said (and by his profession he would be of service to all peoples): "Thou art the Christ, the Son of the living God," not undeservedly he was called "blessed" by the Lord and derived from the word *rock* that solidity associated with his virtue and his name. It was Peter who, through the revelation of the Father, professed that Christ and the Son of God were the same.

ST. AUGUSTINE:

Confessions

I sought a way to obtain the strength which would be capable of enjoying Thee. I did not find it until I embraced the "Mediator between God and man, the man Christ Jesus, who is above all things, God blessed forever," who calls out and says: "I am the Way, the Truth and the Life;" who combined the Food, which I was too weak to take, with flesh–for the Word was made flesh–in order that Thy wisdom, by which Thou has created all things, might become milk for our infancy.

I was not yet humble enough to embrace as my God the humble Jesus, nor did I know what lesson His weakness could teach us. For, Thy Word, the eternal Truth, dwelling in supereminence above the highest parts of Thy creation, has elevated unto Himself those who are subject to Him. And in the lower parts, He has built Himself a humble home from our slime, so that He could detach those, who are to come under it, from themselves and bring them over to Himself, curing their pride and nourishing their love, so that they would advance no further in confidence in themselves, but, rather,

Excerpts from Book Seven, chapters 18 and 19 and Book Four, chapter 12 grow weak, seeing at their feet the Divinity made weak by participation in the tunic of our skin. Thus wearied, they might cast themselves down to It, while It, raising up, would elevate them.

But I thought differently. I thought of my Lord Christ only as of a man of excellent wisdom, whom no one else could equal. Particularly, since He was born miraculously of a virgin, as an example of holding temporal things in contempt in comparison with the attainment of divine immortality, our real concern, He seemed to have merited very great authority as a teacher. However, what "the Word made flesh" meant as a mystery, I was not yet able even to suspect. I had found out only this much about Him from those writings which had been handed down: that He ate and drank, slept, walked, became joyful and sorrowful, engaged in conversation, and that this flesh could not have united to Thy Word, without a human soul and mind. Every man knows this already who knows the immutability of Thy Word.

I knew this insofar as I was able, nor did I have any doubt at all on that score. Indeed, to move the members of the body through the will on one occasion, and not to move them on another; to be affected by some feeling at one time and not to be affected at another time; now to express wise views and now to remain in silence—these belong to the mutability of the soul and mind. And if these things written about Him were false, then all would be threatened by falsehood, and no saving faith in these writings would remain for mankind. So, since these things which are written are true, I recognized the whole man in Christ; not just the body of man, or a soul in the body but without a mind, but man himself. And I thought that He was set above all others, not by the very nature of truth, but by the singular excellence of His human nature and His more perfect participation in wisdom.

But I admit that it was only some time later that I learned to distinguish the Catholic truth. This Life of ours came down here and took up our death and slew it from the abundance of His own life. He has thundered forth the summons for us to return from here to Him, into that hidden place, whence He first proceeded to us into that virginal womb, wherein the human creature was wedded to Him. And from thence, like a bridegroom proceeding from his bedchamber, he bounded forth as a giant to run his course. Nor did He delay, but ran along, crying out by words, by deeds, by death, by life, by descending, by ascending—crying out that we must return to Him.

He disappeared from before our eyes so that we might return into our heart and find Him. He has departed and, behold, He is here. He did not wish to stay long with us, yet He did not abandon us. He went away to that place which He never left; for the world was made by Him, and He was in the world, and He came into the world to save sinners.

Ecclesiastical History

It is now time to show that the very name of Jesus, and especially that of Christ, had already been honored by the ancient God-loving prophets. Moses himself, having been the first to make known the name of Christ as being especially revered and glorious, having handed down the types and symbols of heavenly things and the mysterious images. He consecrated a man High Priest of God, insofar as it was at all possible and called this man "Christ"; that is, to this dignity of the High Priesthood which with him surpassed all pre-eminence among men, for additional honor and glory he attaches the name of Christ.

The same Moses also foresaw by divine inspiration the name Jesus very clearly, and again also endowed this with special privilege. The name of Jesus, which had never been uttered among men before it was made known to Moses, Moses applied first to the one who would rule after his death, whom he knew would also be a type and symbol of our Savior. And in this way, Moses bestowed the name of our Savior as a mark of the greatest honor,

Excerpts from Book One, Chapter 3

upon the two men who in his mind surpassed all the rest of the people in honor and glory—the high priest and him who would rule after him.

And the prophets of succeeding times also clearly foretold Christ by name, giving testimony before hand both to the intrigue of the people who were destined to rise against Him, and to the calling of the Gentiles through Him. At one time David says in perplexity thus: "Why have the Gentiles raged, and the people devised vain things? The kings of the earth stood up, and the princes met together, against the Lord, and against His Christ," to which he later adds in the person of Christ Himself: "The Lord hath said to me: 'Thou art my son, this day have I begotten thee. Ask of me and I will give thee the Gentiles for thy inheritance and the utmost parts of the earth for thy possession.'"

Now the name of Christ (Anointed) adorned not only those among the Hebrews who were honored with the poured oil as a symbol, but also the kings whom the prophets at the bidding of God anointed, and, as it were, constituted typical Christs, since they also bore in themselves the types of the royal and sovereign power of the only and true Christ, the divine Word who rules over all. We have also learned that some of the prophets themselves had already through anointing become Christs in type, so that all these have reference to the true

Christ, the divine and heavenly Word, who is the only High Priest of all, the only King of all creation, and the Father's Archprophet of the prophets.

For He received the symbol and types of the High Priesthood from no man, and He did not derive His earthly origin from a race of priests, and He was not elevated to a kingdom by armed forces of men, nor was he like the ancient prophets; He was adorned with truth, not symbols. He is called Christ more than any of these, and as the only true Christ of God Himself, He filled the whole world with Christians, His truly reverend and holy name, handing down to us no longer types or images, but the uncovered virtues themselves and the heavenly life in the very doctrines of truth. He has received the chrism, not that prepared with material substances, but the very divine anointing itself with the spirit of God, by sharing in the unbegotten divinity of the Father.

And Isaias teaches this very truth, exclaiming in one place as if from Christ Himself: "The Spirit of the Lord is upon me. Wherefore he hath anointed me; to preach the gospel to the poor, he hath sent me to announce deliverance to captives and sight to the blind." And not only Isaias, but also David proclaims to His Person, saying: "Thy throne, O God, is forever and ever: the sceptre of thy kingdom is a sceptre of uprightness. Thou hast loved justice and hated iniquity: therefore God, thy God, hath anointed thee with the oil of gladness above thy fellows."

Elsewhere, the same David makes this statement about Him, speaking clearly as follows: "The Lord said to my Lord: Sit thou at my right hand: Until I make thy enemies the footstool of thy feet," and "From the womb before the day star I begot thee. The Lord hath sworn, and he will not repent: Thou art a priest forever according to the order of Melchisedech." Melchisedech is introduced in the Holy Scriptures as a priest of the most high God, not consecrated by any materially prepared oil, and not even as belonging by racial descent to the priesthood of the Hebrews.

Thus according to His order and not that of others who received symbols and types, our Savior has been called Christ and priest with an appeal to an oath. Thus, also, the narrative does not tell us that He was anointed corporeally or that He was of a tribe that held the priesthood, but that He came into being from God Himself before the day star, that is, before the establishment of the world, and that He possesses an immortal and ageless priesthood to boundless eternity.

He is glorified as the only and true High Priest of God, and above all this, as the pre-existent Word of God, who came into being before all ages and received the honor of worship from the Father, is worshipped as God. We who have consecrated ourselves to Him honor Him not only with our voices and with the sound of words, but also with the entire disposition of our soul, so as to prefer giving testimony to Him rather than saving our lives.

Chapter 2

EMMANUEL!

Therefore the Lord himself
shall give you a sign. Behold,
a Virgin shall conceive, and
bear a Son, and call his name
Emmanuel.

Isaias 7:14

Emmanuel, the name meaning God-with-us, expresses the sublime love with which the Father has first loved us. For even a glimpse at the mystery of the Trinity, as seen by reading about the Word, might be so awesome that we could be discouraged in our efforts to seek God. Yet, in the divine economy of our salvation, God comes first to seek us, to offer His love as an encouragement and a reward for our love.

48

God comes, not in the majesty of His power, but in the littleness of a beautiful baby. In the mystery of Christmas the magnificence of the Incarnation is presented to us with such gentleness that we can approach this God who delights to be with the children of men. We can draw near with confidence to this throne of grace, a manger in a stable, unafraid to offer our life and our love.

The vehemence of such divine love that pours itself out at Bethlehem beggars description. Is it any wonder that Abbot Marmion says we can only lisp when we speak of divinity? Saints and scholars and poets search for ways to express this indescribable eminence of ineffable divine love. Yes, we must even coin new words, such as "ineffable", in our attempt to appreciate the length and depth and breadth of God's love.

But speaking through the prophet, centuries ago, God described His love for us in a word—Emmanuel—God-with-us!

49

ST. JUSTIN, MARTYR:

The First Apology

The Prophet Isaias spoke thus: "A star shall rise out of Jacob and a flower shall spring from the root of Jesse, and in His arm shall nations trust." Indeed a brilliant star has arisen, and a flower has sprung up from the root of Jesse—this is Christ. For by God's power He was conceived by a virgin who was a descendant of Jacob, who was the father of Juda, the father of the Jewish race; and Jesse was His forefather according to this prophecy, and He was the son of Jacob and Juda according to lineage.

And again, hear how it was expressly foretold by Isaias that He was to be born of a virgin. Here is the prophecy: "Behold a virgin shall conceive and bear a son, and His name shall be called Emmanuel" (i.e. God with us). For, what man has deemed incredible and impossible, God foretold through Prophetic Spirit as about to take place, so that, when they take place, they should not be denied, but believed, because they had been foretold.

Let us attempt to explain the words of the prophecy. The words "Behold a virgin shall conceive" therefore mean that the virgin shall conceive without intercourse. For if she had had intercourse

Excerpts from chapters 32, 33, and 34.

with anyone whomsoever, she was no longer a virgin, but the power of God descending upon the virgin overshadowed her and caused her, while still a virgin, to conceive. And the angel of God who was then sent to that same virgin, carried the glad news to her when he said: "Behold, thou shalt conceive in thy womb of the Holy Spirit, and shalt bring forth a Son, and He shall be called the Son of the Most High, and thou shalt call His name Jesus, for He shall deliver His people from their sins."

This happened as related by the recorders of all the acts of our Savior Jesus Christ, whom we believed, and through the above-mentioned Isaias the Prophetic Spirit foretold that He should be born in the manner we stated above. And it was this Spirit who came upon the virgin, overshadowed her, and brought it about that she became pregnant, not by sexual intercourse, but by divine power.

Jesus is a name in the Hebrew tongue which means Savior in the Greek; thus the angel said to the virgin: "And thou shalt call His name Jesus, for He shall deliver His people from their sins."

And hear in what part of this earth He was to be born, as it was foretold by another Prophet, Micheas, who spoke thus: "And thou, Bethlehem, land of Juda, art not the least among the princes of Juda; for out of thee shall come forth a ruler, who shall free my people." Now this Bethlehem is a certain village in the land of the Jews, distant thirty-five stadia from Jerusalem, where Jesus Christ was born, as you can learn by consulting the census taken by Quirinius, the first procurator in Judea.

ST. LEO THE GREAT:

The Testimony

And He came to earth and proceeded as a man from the Virgin's womb, which He sanctified. Confirming by this process the interpretation of His name, Emmanuel, that is, "God with us," He began in a marvelous way to be what we are and did not cease to be what He was. He assumed our nature in such a way as not to lose what He Himself was. Although John writes, "The Word was made flesh" (that is, in other words, 'man'), He was not turned into flesh, since He never ceased to be God.

And the holy David says to Him: "Thou art always the self-same." Indeed, the Father bears witness from heaven and says, "Thou art my beloved Son, in Thee I am well pleased." Thus, having become also a man, He is said according to our profession, to remain what He was before man was made. Paul preaches the same as we do: "Jesus Christ is the same, yesterday and today and forever." He shows in what he says that Christ did not change His original nature and did not lessen the riches of His divinity because He took on the full likeness of our condition, being made poor on our account.

Excerpts from Letter 165

The one Son of the Father and our Mediator neither lost His equality nor was separated from association with us: the invisible God and visible man hidden in the nature of a slave, and the Lord of glory, acknowledged in the profession of those who believe. The Father did not deprive Him of title to His nature after He was made man, and a poor one, on our behalf. And at the Baptism in the Jordan River the Father called Him His only-begotten Son, not by any other title. "Thou art my beloved Son, in whom I am well pleased." Neither was our likeness changed into the nature of divinity, nor was divinity changed into the likeness of our nature.

He was called a man, for (although He is by nature God, the Word of God the Father) He shared in flesh and blood, as we do. That is the way He manifested Himself to those on the earth, not losing what He was, but taking on the nature of a man, complete in respect to itself.

He is therefore one: before the Incarnation the true God, and who in His humanity remained what He was, and is, and will be. The one Lord Jesus Christ, therefore, is not to be divided, into man on the one side, and God on the other. We say that Jesus Christ is one and the same—not being unaware of the differences in the natures, but keeping them distinct from each other.

The Baptism of Jesus (particular), GIOTTO
Chapel of the Scrovegni, Padua

"The Father did not deprive Him of title to His nature
after He was made man, and a poor one, on our behalf.
And at the baptism in the Jordan River the Father called Him
His only-begotten Son, not by any other title. 'Thou art my
beloved Son, in whom I am well pleased.' "

ST. LEO THE GREAT

When, therefore, God came forth from the Virgin in that human nature which He assumed, being made one out of two elements opposed to each other, that is, of flesh and spirit, the one element is taken up into God, the other dispenses the grace of God. He was indeed sent, but as a man, for there were two natures in Him. In fact, it was as a man that He wearied from travel, He was hungry and thirsted, and became sad and wept, according to the regular custom of human bodies.

We see certain qualities in Christ so human that they do not appear to differ in any way from the common frailty of mortals, and certain qualities so divine that they are suited to no other nature than to the ineffable nature of God. And on that account man's limited intelligence is in a quandary, benumbed by so great an admiration. It does not know where to turn, what to hold, whither to betake itself.

If it thinks Him a man, it notices Him returning from the dead with spoils, having overcome the realm of death. For this reason we must contemplate with all fear and reverence how the reality of both natures is shown to exist in one and the same Person in such a way that nothing unworthy or unbecoming may be thought about the divine and ineffable nature, and, again the deeds performed as a man may not be considered as ridiculed by false representations.

And so He was born of the Father before all ages and came forth in the flesh from a woman. This was not because His divine nature took its start from the holy Virgin, and not because the divinity undertook the work of a second birth on its own account after the birth which He received from His Father. No, it was because He joined a human nature to Himself and came forth from a woman, and is therefore said to have been born in the flesh on our account and for our salvation. It was not that He was first born as an ordinary man from the holy Virgin and then the Word began to dwell in Him afterwards; He joined flesh to Himself in the very matrix and womb of the Virgin, and underwent carnal birth, making His own the nativity of His flesh.

This is to show that the Word of God, just as we do, participated in flesh and blood and that our body was His very own, and that as a man He came forth from a woman without casting aside or putting off His divinity or that birth which He had from the Father; but even in the assuming of the flesh He remained God as He was. This is the explanation of the correct belief as it is everywhere stated. We have just seen that the Fathers teach this.

Hence, they did not hesitate to call the holy Virgin "Mother of God," not because the nature of the Word and the Godhead took their origin in the holy Virgin, but because from her was born the sacred body animated with a rational soul; substantially united to which the Word of God is said to have been born in the flesh.

ST. PETER CHRYSOLOGUS:

The Annunciation

Dearly beloved, our present desire should be to have eyes sufficiently strong and penetrating to look upon the brilliance of a divine origin. Even when our bodily eyes are fully sound and well-preserved, they can scarcely endure the radiance of the rising sun. What firm strength, then, must we prepare for our interior vision, to enable it to gaze upon the splendor of its rising and brilliant Creator?

"Now in the sixth month," we read, "the angel Gabriel was sent to a town of Galilee called Nazareth, to a virgin betrothed to a man named Joseph." The holy Evangelist points out the place, the time, and the person, that the truths of his account may receive confirmation from the clear evidence furnished by the very details he sets down.

"The angel was sent to a betrothed virgin." To this virgin God sends a winged messenger. He who bears this gift of grace is giving her a pledge, and he is carrying back a dowry from her. He receives her promise, and hands over to her the gifts of God's overshadowing power—he who sets free the promise of the virgin's consent. The swift mediator flies in haste to the maiden, to keep away the completion

Excerpts from sermon 140.

of her human engagement from the spouse of God, and to hold it in suspension. He does this, not to take the virgin away from Joseph, but to restore her to Christ, to whom she was pledged when she was beginning to exist in the womb. Christ, then, receives His own spouse; He does not take away the spouse of another. Neither does He cause the breaking of an engagement with someone else when He unites her, His creature, exclusively to Himself in one body.

But let us hear what the angel did. "When the angel had come to her, he said: 'Hail, full of grace, the Lord is with thee.'" The salutation contains a giving, a giving of a present, and not merely an expression of greeting. "Ave!" "Hail!" This means: receive grace. Do not be alarmed or worried about your nature. "O maiden full of grace!" Grace exists even in other men. Surely, then, the whole fullness of grace will come upon you.

"The Lord is with thee." Why is the Lord with you? Because He is coming down into you in a new mystery, that of being born. Fittingly did the angel add: "Blessed art thou among women." Through the curse she incurred Eve brought pains upon the wombs of women in childbirth. Now in this very matter of motherhood, Mary, through the blessing she received, rejoices, is honored, is exalted. Now, too, womankind has become truly the mother of those who live through grace, just as previously she was the mother of those who by nature are subject to death.

"But when she had seen him she was troubled at his word." Why is it that she gazes upon her angelic visitor, but it is only at his word that she is troubled? Because the angel had come as one of pleasing appearance, strong in war, meek in his bearing, terrible in his speech, uttering human words but promising things divine. The presence of the one sent had moved her but slightly, but the authority of the Sender struck her with full force.

She soon realized that she was receiving within herself the Judge, there in that same place where with lingering gaze she had just seen the messenger from heaven. It was with holy affection that God transformed the virgin into a mother for Himself, and made His handmaid into a parent. Nevertheless, her bosom was disturbed, her mind recoiled, and her whole state became one of trembling when God, whom the whole of creation does not contain, placed His whole Self inside her bosom and made Himself a man.

"And she kept pondering," the Scripture continues, "what manner of greeting this might be." Notice that the virgin gave her consent not to a greeting of mere words, but to the realities of which they told her. Notice, too, that the salutation was not one of ordinary courtesy; rather, it contained the full might of heavenly power. So she gives the matter careful thought. For to make hasty replies is characteristic of human levity, to think deeply is the mark of the greatest constancy and of judgment fully mature. The man who sees no reason to be astonished at her attitude or to marvel at her spirit does not truly know how great God is.

Before Him the vault of heaven shakes and the angels tremble. No creature bears Him up, nor can all nature bound Him. Yet this one young maiden takes Him into an inner chamber of repose, her womb. She receives Him, and delights Him with her hospitality. Thus she gives Him a dwelling that she may request in payment, and get as the price for use of her very womb, peace for the earth, glory for heaven, salvation for the lost, life for the dead, for those on earth relationship with the saints—even union of God Himself with man. She does all this, too, to fulfill the Prophet's statement: "Behold, the inheritance of the Lord are children: the reward, the fruit of the womb."

ST. JUSTIN, MARTYR:

Dialogue with Trypho

So also was the prophecy beginning with the words, "Behold a virgin shall conceive and bear a son," spoken of Him. For if the one of whom Isaias spoke was not to be born of a virgin, to whom did the Holy Spirit allude when He said: "Behold, the Lord Himself shall give you a sign: Behold, a virgin shall conceive and bear a Son"?

If He was to be born of human intercourse like any other first-born son, why did God solemnly announce that He would give a sign which is not common to all first-born? What is truly a sign, and what was to be an irrefutable proof to all men, namely, that by means of a virgin's womb the First-born of all creatures took flesh and truly became man, was foreknown by the Prophetic Spirit before it took place and foretold by Him in different ways. Indeed, He foretold this in order that, when it did take place, everyone would understand that it all happened by the power and purpose of the Creator of the world.

Then, at the time of His birth, the Magi came from Arabia and worshipped Him, after they had met Herod, then King of that country, whom Scrip-

Excerpts from chapters 63, 77, 78, and 84

ture calls the king of Assyria because of his wicked ungodliness. At the time when the Magi from Arabia came to King Herod and said, "From the star which has appeared in the heavens we know that a King has been born in your country, and we have come to worship Him," he asked the elders of your people and learned from them that Christ was to be born in Bethlehem.

For they replied that it was written in the Prophet, "And thou, Bethlehem, in the land of Juda, art by no means least among the princes of Juda; for out of thee shall come a Ruler who shall shepherd My people." Now, these Magi from Arabia came to Bethlehem, worshipped the Child, and presented to Him gifts of gold, frankincense and myrrh. After they had worshipped Him in Bethlehem, they were admonished in a vision not to return to Herod.

And Joseph, the spouse of Mary, who at first had decided to put her away because he thought she was pregnant through human intercourse, namely, fornication, was likewise commanded in a vision not to do so, when the angel appeared to him and told him that what she had conceived was of the Holy Spirit. Consequently, overwhelmed with awe, he did not put her away.

But when Quirinius was taking his first census in Judea, Joseph traveled from Nazareth, where he lived, to Bethlehem, to which he belonged, to be enrolled, for he was by birth of the tribe of Juda, which inhabited that region. Then he was ordered in a vision to go with Mary into Egypt and to remain there with the Child until another revelation should advise them to return to Judea.

Now, concerning the birth of the Child in Bethlehem, when Joseph could find no lodging place in the village, he went to a cave nearby, and there Mary gave birth to the Child and laid Him in a manger. There the Arabian Magi found Him. Now, when the Magi failed to return to Herod as he had requested, but had gone to their own country by another route, as they had been ordered, and when Joseph, Mary and the Child had already retired into Egypt, as they were divinely directed, Herod, since he did not know who the Child was whom the Magi had come to worship, ordered every boy in Bethlehem without exception to be slain.

This, too, had been foretold, by Jeremias, when the Holy Spirit spoke through him in this fashion: "A voice was heard in Rama, weeping and great lamentation; Rachel weeping for her children, and refusing to be comforted for them, because they are not." Therefore, because of the voice which was to be heard as far as Rama, that is, as far as Arabia (for even today there is a place in Arabia called Rama), lamentation was to fill the place where Rachel (the wife of the holy Patriarch Jacob, whose name was later changed to Israel) lies buried, that is, Bethlehem, for the women were weeping for their massacred children and had no consolation for that which had occurred.

And to continue the words of Isaias: "Who shall declare His generation? For His life is taken from earth," seems to indicate that He, who is said to be consigned to death by God because of the sins of the people, did not have mere human origin. Moses, too, in speaking of His blood in a formerly quoted parable, said: "He shall wash His robe in the blood of the grape," since His blood did not originate from human seed but from the will of God.

And then, there are the words of David: "In the brightness of Thy saints, from the womb before the day star I begot Thee. The Lord hath sworn, and He will not repent: Thou art a Priest forever according to the order of Melchisedech." Do not these words signify that from ancient times God, the Father of all things, intended Him to be begotten again and of a human womb?

In another passage previously cited, He says: "Thy throne, O God, is forever and ever; the sceptre of Thy kingdom is a sceptre of uprightness. Thou hast loved justice and hated iniquity; therefore God, Thy God, hath anointed Thee with the oil of gladness above Thy fellows. Kings' daughters are (gathered) in Thy honor. The queen stood at Thy right hand, in gilded clothing, surrounded with variety. Hearken, O daughter, and see, and incline thy ear, and forget thy people and thy father's house. And the king shall greatly desire thy beauty, for He is thy Lord, and Him thou shalt adore."

These words show clearly that He who did all things (God the Father) testified that He (Jesus) is to be worshipped both as God and Christ. They further show that the Word of God speaks to His faithful (who are of one soul and one synagogue and one church) as to a daughter, namely, the Church which was established by and partakes of His name, for we are all called Christians. That this is so, and that we are instructed to forget the ancient customs of our ancestors, the following words imply: "Hearken, O daughter, and see, and incline thy ear, and forget thy people and thy father's house; and the king shall greatly desire thy beauty, for He is thy Lord, and Him thou shalt adore."

ST. JOHN DAMASCENE:

The Orthodox Faith

After the holy Virgin had given her assent, the Holy Spirit came upon her according to the Lord's word, which the angel had spoken, and purified her, and gave her the power both to receive the divinity of the Word, and to beget Him. Then the subsistent Wisdom and Power of the Most High, the Son of God, the consubstantial with the Father, overshadowed her like a divine seed, and from her most chaste and pure blood compacted for Himself a body animated by a rational and intellectual soul as first-fruits of our clay.

This was not by sperm but by creation, through the Holy Spirit, with the form not being put together but being completed all at once with the Word of God Himself serving as the person to the flesh. For the divine Word was not united to an already self-subsistent flesh, but, without being circumscribed, came in His own Person to dwell in the womb of the holy Virgin. The very Word became person to the body!

Thus, there was a body which was at once the body of God the Word and an animate, rational, intellectual body. Therefore, we do not say that

Excerpts from Book Three, chapters 2-8

man became God, but that God became man. For, while He was by nature perfect God, the same became by nature perfect man. He did not change His nature and neither did He just appear to become man.

On the contrary, without confusion or alteration or division He became hypostatically united to the rationally and intellectually animated flesh which He had from the holy Virgin and which had its existence in Him. He did not transform the nature of His divinity into the substance of His flesh, nor the substance of His flesh into the nature of His divinity, and neither did He effect one compound nature out of His divine nature and the human nature which He had assumed.

The natures were united to each other without change and without alteration. The divine nature did not give up its proper simplicity, and the human nature was certainly not changed into the nature of the divinity, nor did it become non-existent. Neither was there one compound nature made from the two natures. If Christ had one compound nature after the union, then He is neither consubstantial with His Father, who has a simple nature, nor with His Mother, because she was not composed of divinity and humanity. Nor, indeed, would He belong to divinity or humanity, nor could He be called God or man.

We confess that from divinity and humanity there is the same perfect God and that He both is and is said to be of two natures and in two natures. We say that the term 'Christ' is the name of the person and that it is not used in a restricted sense, but as signifying what is of the two natures. Thus He anointed Himself—as God, anointing His body with His divinity—but as man, being anointed, because He is both one and the other. Moreover, the anointing of the humanity is the divinity.

We confess one Person of the Son of God incarnate in two natures that remain perfect, and we declare that the Person of His divinity and of His humanity is the same, and we profess that the two natures are preserved intact in Him after the union. We do not set each nature apart by itself, but hold them to be united to each other in one Person. Thus, that which was created remains created, and that which was uncreated, uncreated; the mortal remained mortal, and the immortal, immortal; the circumscribed remained circumscribed and the uncircumscribed, uncircumscribed; the visible remained visible and the invisible, invisible. As St. Leo says, "The one glows with miracles, while the other has succumbed to insults."

Moreover, the Word makes human things His own, because what is proper to His sacred flesh belongs to Him; and the things which are His own

He communicates to His flesh. This is after the manner of an exchange on account of the mutual immanence of the parts and the hypostatic union, and because He who performed both human and divine acts with each form cooperating, was one and the same Person.

Wherefore, the Lord of Glory is even said to have been crucified, although His divine nature did not suffer; and the Son of Man is confessed to have been in heaven before His passion, as the Lord Himself has said. We recognize both the miracles and the sufferings as His, even though it was in one nature that He worked miracles and in another that He endured suffering.

When we speak of the divinity, we do not attribute the properties of the humanity to it. Thus we never speak of a passible or created divinity. Neither do we predicate the divine properties of the flesh, for we never speak of uncreated flesh or humanity. In the case of the person, however, whether we speak of it from both of the parts or from one of them, we attribute the properties of both the natures to the Person. Thus Christ is called both God and man, created and uncreated.

We say, further, that this divine Person of God the Word exists before all things timelessly and eternally, simple and uncompounded, uncreated, incorporeal, invisible, intangible and uncircumscribed. And we say that He has all things that the Father has, since He is consubstantial with Him, and that He differs from the Person of the Father by the manner of His begetting and by relation; that He is perfect and never leaves the Person of the Father.

But at the same time, we say that in latter times, without leaving the bosom of the Father, the Word came to dwell uncircumscribed in the womb of the holy Virgin, without sperm and without being contained, and in the very same Person as exists before the ages He made flesh subsist for Himself from the holy Virgin.

Thus, He was in all things and above all things, and at the same time He was existing in the womb of the holy Mother of God, but He was there by the operation of the Incarnation. He had those properties of the divine nature in which He is one with the Father and the Spirit, and also had those features of human nature in which He is one with His Mother and with us.

Christ, then, who is perfect God and perfect man, is one. Him do we adore with the Father and the Spirit together with His immaculate body in one adoration. And we do not say that His body is not to be adored, because it is adored in the one

Person of the Word, who became Person to it. We do not adore it as a mere body, but as being one with the divinity because His two natures belong to the one Person of the Word of God. Christ, indeed, who is perfect God and perfect man, is one.

ST. BERNARD:

On the Canticle of Canticles

The Holy Spirit wisely compares the bridegroom's name to oil when He leads the bride to exclaim to the bridegroom: "Your name is as oil poured out." For oil gives light, nourishes, and anoints. Oil kindles fire, renews the flesh and eases pain. It is light, food, and medicine.

How much more so is the name of the true Bridegroom! When preached, His name gives light; when contemplated, it nourishes the soul; when invoked, it heals and eases our wounds. We can profitably meditate upon each point.

Consider how the light of faith was enkindled so brightly, so swiftly, throughout the whole world because the name of Jesus was preached. It is in the light of this name that God has so marvellously called us to His admirable Light. How accurately St. Paul describes us who have been enlightened and who glory in the true Light when he says: "For you were formerly darkness, but now you are light in the Lord."

The same Apostle was commanded to carry this Name before kings and Gentiles and the chil-

Excerpts from Sermon 15

74

dren of Israel. Indeed, he carried this Name to the world as a light and illuminated his own country, crying out everywhere: "The night is passed and the day is at hand. Let us therefore cast aside the works of darkness and put on the armor of light. Let us walk honestly as in the daylight."

He showed everyone the candle on the candlestick, everywhere preaching Jesus, and Him crucified. How resplendent was that light! How dazzling to the eye of the beholder! When it thundered forth from the lips of St. Peter, it cured the man who was lame, and like lightning it illuminated the spiritually blind. Did he not cast fire on the earth when he cried out: "In the name of Jesus Christ of Nazareth, rise and walk!"

The name of Jesus is not only light, but it is also food. Are you not strengthened as often as you call it to mind? What else so strengthens the soul of the person contemplating it! What else so renews our tired senses, encourages us to virtue, establishes good and holy habits and develops noble affections? All spiritual consolation dries up unless infused with this oil; it all becomes insipid unless seasoned with this salt. If someone writes a book, I cannot savor it unless it speaks to me of Jesus. If someone speaks or preaches, I cannot enjoy it unless I find Jesus therein.

The name of Jesus is honey in the mouth, music to the ear, a cry of gladness in the heart!

Is there someone sad among us? Let him invite Jesus into his heart and let the name spring to his lips. Indeed, it is medicine. With the dawn of that name every cloud disappears and peace returns. Has someone among us fallen deep into sin? Is he rushing toward the precipice? If he invoke the name of Life, he will be drawn back to life.

PRUDENTIUS:

Hymns

Unveil Thy sweetness, Child divine,
The fruit of virgin motherhood
And chastity inviolate,
Our Mediator, God and man.
Though Thou didst come from the mouth of God,
Born as His Word on earth below,
Yet as His Wisdom Thou didst live
Forever in the Father's Heart.
Until the slow revolving years
In centuries at length had passed,
And He Himself vouchsafed to come
Down to the world grown old in sin.
Yet such destruction of mankind
The Heart of Christ could not endure;
And lest His Father's handiwork,
Unvindicated should be lost,
He clothed Himself in mortal flesh,
That by arising from the tomb
He might unlock the chains of death
And bring man to His Father's house.
The Infant's feeble cry proclaimed
The springtime of the universe;

Excerpts from *A Hymn for Christmas Day*

The world reborn then cast aside
The gloom of winter's lethargy.

This is Thy natal day, on which
The high Creator sent Thee forth,
And gave to Thee a form of clay,
Uniting flesh with His own Word.

Are you aware, O Virgin blest,
As weary months of waiting end,
That your untarnished purity
Shines brighter in your Motherhood?

At Thy Nativity, O Child,
All hard unfeeling things were stirred;
The unrelenting crags grew kind
And clothed in flinty stones with grass.

Now from the rocks sweet honey flows;
Now fragrant liquor is distilled
From shrivelled trunks of aged oaks,
And tamarisks yield ambrosial balms.

Chapter 3

THE
SON
OF
MAN

And Jesus advanced in wisdom
and age and grace
before God and man.

Luke 2:52

Today, when a priest is giving instructions, he seldom meets anyone who denies or questions the humanity of Christ. The proof seems so obvious: Christ ate and drank and slept; He grew in wisdom and age and grace; He wept over Lazarus and over Jerusalem; He prayed; He even died. The vital manliness of Christ emerges from His words and works, admirable and imitable.

79

However, the pagan world of the Roman Empire in which the Church first exercised its mission, was a world almost over-crowded with gods. Anything or anyone extraordinary or un-usual could be deified. Many of these people did not object to a new god coming out of Palestine, but they did consider it unworthy to call Him a man, too. His cross was indeed a stum-bling block, for no god must die.

So the work of the early Church was twofold. It must be proven that there was only one God, and that Jesus Christ was the Son of God, and it must be demonstrated that He was also truly a man. Even aside from the tremendous significance of the title "Son of Man" in its prophetic and Messianic dignity, it also enunciated the dogma that a perfect human nature had been assumed by the Son of God.

This One Person, called the Word or the Son, has two perfect natures. One is divine, so that this Person is truly the Son of God; the other is human, so that this Person is truly the son of Mary. This "personal" or Hypostatic union must be taught for an understanding of the Incarnation, the mystery of the Word-made-flesh.

How truly Jesus is Lord—our God, our Brother!

EUSEBIUS:

Ecclesiastical History

My work will begin with the dispensation conceived in relation to Christ and the divinity ascribed to Him, loftier and greater than human
conception. For, he who intends to hand down in
writing the story of the Church's leadership must
begin with the very origin of Christ's dispensation
itself, divine indeed, from whom we lay claim to
our name, Christian.

Since His nature is twofold—on the one hand
like the head of the body whereby He is recognized
as God; on the other, comparable to the feet whereby He put on man of like nature with ourselves for
the sake of our salvation—our account of subsequent
events therefore would be complete only if we
should begin with the story of the most capital
and lordly events of His entire history.

Now, no language would be sufficient for a
description of the origin and the dignity and the
very substance and nature of Christ, just as indeed,
the Holy Spirit says in the prophecies: "Who shall
declare his generation?" for no one knows the
Father except the Son, nor in turn, does anyone

Excerpts from Book One, Chapters 1 and 2

ever know the Son worthily except the Father alone, who begot Him. And who except the Father could clearly conceive the Light that existed before the world, and the Wisdom that was intellectual and essential before the ages, the living Word who was in the beginning God by the side of the Father, the first and only offspring of God before all creation and making both visible and invisible, the commander-in-chief of the rational and immortal host of heaven.

He is the angel of great counsel, the promoter of the ineffable plan, together with the Father the maker of all things, the true and only-begotten Son of God, the Lord and God and King of all things begotten, who has received at once lordship and power with divinity itself and might and honor from the Father, for according to the mystical passages of the Scriptures which deal with His divinity: "In the beginnng was the Word, and the Word was with God; and the Word was God; all things were made through him, and without him was made nothing."

And that there is a certain living and subsisting substance who ministered to the Father and God of the universe for the making of all created things called the Word and Wisdom, can be learned from the very person of Wisdom, who through Solomon somewhat thus reveals the mysteries concerning itself: "I wisdom dwell in counsel and am present in learned thoughts. By me kings reign, and the mighty decree justice; by me great men are magnified and princes rule the earth by me." And to this is added: "In the beginning before making the earth, before the fountains of water sprang up, before the mountains had been established, and before all the hills, he brought me forth. When he prepared the heavens, I was present with him, and when he made safe the fountains under the heavens, I was with him disposing them." So, let this be our proof in brief that the divine Word pre-existed.

At the beginning of the Roman Empire, there appeared to all men and to the Gentiles throughout the world, as if previously assisted and now actually ready for the reception of the knowledge of the Father, that same teacher of the virtues, the assistant of the Father in all good things, the divine and heavenly Word of God, in a human body in no way different from the substance of our own nature.

And He performed and suffered such things as were in accord with the prophecies which foretold that One who was both man and God would come to dwell in the world, as the performer of miraculous deeds, and that He would be made manifest to all the Gentiles as the teacher of the worship of the

Father, and that the marvels of His birth and His new teaching and the wonder of His deeds, and, in addition to these, the manner of His death and resurrection from the dead, and above all, His divine Ascension into heaven would also be manifest.

ST. IGNATIUS OF ANTIOCH:

Letters

I offer up my life as a poor substitute for the Cross, which is a stumbling block to those who have no faith, but to us salvation and eternal life. Where is the wise man? Where is the philosopher? Where is the boasting of the so-called men of prudence? For our God Jesus Christ was, according to God's dispensation, the fruit of Mary's womb, of the seed of David; He was born and baptized in order that He might make the water holy by His passion.

The maidenhood of Mary and her childbearing and also the death of the Lord were hidden from the prince of this world—three resounding mysteries wrought in the silence of God. How, then, did He appear in time? A star, brighter than all other stars, shone in the sky, and its brightness was ineffable and the novelty of it caused astonishment. And the rest of the stars, along with the sun and the moon, formed a choir about the star; but the light of the star by itself outshone all the rest.

It was a puzzle to know the origin of this novelty unlike anything else. Thereupon all magic was dissolved, every bond of malice disappeared, ignor-

Excerpts from the *Letter to the Ephesians,* and passim, from the other letters.

ance was destroyed, the ancient kingdom was ruined, when God appeared in the form of man to give us newness of eternal life. What had been prepared in God now had a beginning. And, because of the plan of the abolition of death, all things were disturbed.

In a second letter which I intend to write you, I shall explain more fully what I have merely touched upon—the dispensation of becoming the new man Jesus Christ, who is of the race of David according to the passion and resurrection. Come together in common, one and all without exception in charity, in one faith and in one Jesus Christ, who is of the race of David according to the flesh, the son of man and Son of God, so that with undivided mind you may obey the bishop and the priests, and break one Bread which is the medicine of immortality and the antidote against death, enabling us to live forever in Jesus Christ.

Be zealous, then, in the observance of one Eucharist. For there is one flesh of our Lord, Jesus Christ, and one chalice that brings union in His Blood. There is one altar, as there is one bishop with the priests and deacons, who are my fellow workers. And so, whatever you do, let it be done in the name of God.

Desire within me has been nailed to the cross and no flame of material longing is left. Only the living water speaks within me saying: Hasten to the Father. I have no taste for the food that perishes nor for the pleasures of this life. I want the Bread of God which is the Flesh of Christ, and for drink I desire His Blood, which is love that cannot be destroyed.

For there is one Doctor active in both body and soul, begotten and yet unbegotten, God in man, true life in death, son of Mary and Son of God, first able to suffer and then unable to suffer, Jesus Christ our Lord.

And so, be deaf when anyone speaks to you apart from Jesus Christ, who was of the race of David, the son of Mary, who was truly born and ate and drank, who was truly persecuted under Pontius Pilate and was really crucified and died in the sight of those "in heaven and on the earth and under the earth." Moreover He was truly raised from the dead by the power of His Father; in like manner His Father, through Jesus Christ, will raise up those of us who believe in Him. Apart from Him we have no true life.

ST. LEO THE GREAT:

Letter to Emperor Leo

Whoever, then, are so blinded and so estranged from the light as to deny the reality of human flesh in the Word of God from the moment of the Incarnation on, ought to show what right they have for using the title of Christians. They should show by what process of reasoning they are in agreement with the Gospel of truth in their claim that, when the blessed Virgin gave birth, there was produced either flesh without divinity or divinity without flesh. As it is impossible to deny that, according to the Evangelist's words, "The Word was made flesh and dwelt among us," so it is impossible to deny that, according to the teaching of blessed Paul the Apostle, "God was in Christ, reconciling the world to himself."

What reconciliation could there be in which God might again be made propitious to the human race if the Mediator between God and men did not take upon Himself the cause of all men? How, indeed, might anyone fulfill the reality of a mediator unless he shared in the nature of God, equal to the

Excerpts from letter 261

Father, and also in our servile nature, so that the bonds of death, brought about by the sin of one person, might be loosed by the death of One who alone was in no way subject to death?

The outpouring of Christ's blood for sinners was so rich in value that, if all the enslaved believed in their Redeemer, none of them would be held by the chains of the devil. For, as the Apostle says, "Where the offense has abounded, grace has abounded yet more." And since those born under the sentence of original sin have received the power of rebirth unto justification, the gift of freedom became stronger than the debt of slavery.

Consequently, what hope do they leave themselves in the refuge of this mystery who deny the reality of the human body in our Savior? Let them say by what sacrifice they have become reconciled. Let them say by what blood they have been redeemed. Who is there, as the Apostle says, that "has delivered himself up for us an offering and a sacrifice to God to ascend in fragrant odor?" Or what sacrifice was ever more holy than that which the true and eternal Priest placed upon the altar of the Cross by the immolation of His own flesh?

Although the death of many holy people was precious in the sight of the Lord, the redemption of the world was not effected by the killing of any of these guiltless persons. The just received crowns;

they did not give them. From the courage of the faithful came examples of patience, not the gifts of justification. Indeed, their individual deaths affected them individually, and none gave his life to pay another's debt.

For among the sons of men only one stood out, our Lord Jesus Christ, who was truly the spotless Lamb, in whose person all were crucified, all died, all were buried, all were raised from the dead. He Himself said about them: "And I, if I be lifted up from the earth, will draw all things to myself." Indeed, true faith, justifying the impious and making just men, being drawn to Him who shares in their human nature, receives salvation in Him in whom alone man finds himself without guilt. And it can freely boast, through God's grace, of the power of Him who in the lowliness of our flesh attacked the enemy of the human race and who turned over His victory to those in whose body He triumphed.

It is true, therefore, that there is in the one Lord Jesus Christ, the true Son of God and man, one Person of the Word and the flesh, and without separation and division, they perform their acts in common. Still, we must understand the character of the acts themselves and must note, by the contemplation of pure faith, to which acts the lowliness of the flesh is elevated, to which acts the heights of Divinity bend down; what the flesh does not per-

Cure of the Blind Man (particular), Duccio
National Gallery, London

"Without the power of the Word there would be no curing
of the infirm, no restoration of life to the dead."

ST. LEO THE GREAT

form apart from the Word, what the Word apart from the flesh does not effect.

Without the power of the Word the Virgin would not conceive, nor give birth; and without the reality of the flesh the infant would not lie wrapped in swaddling clothes. Without the power of the Word the Magi would not adore the boy pointed out to them by the guiding star, and without the reality of the flesh there would be no command to transfer the boy into Egypt and remove Him from Herod's persecution.

Without the power of the Word the voice of the Father from heaven would not say: "This is my beloved Son, in whom I am well pleased." And without the reality of the flesh John would not exclaim: "Behold the Lamb of God, behold Him who takes away the sin of the world." Without the power of the Word there would be no curing of the infirm, no restoration of life to the dead, and without reality of flesh there would be no need to eat when hungry or sleep when tired. Finally, without the power of the Word the Lord could not claim to be equal to the Father, and without the reality of the flesh He would not say that the Father was greater than He.

For both are accepted and defended by the Catholic faith, which, according to the profession of the blessed Apostle Peter, believes in one Christ, the Son of the living God, both man and Word. Hence it is true that, from the beginning when "the Word was made flesh," in the womb of the Virgin, there never existed any division between the two natures, and during the entire growth of His body, His acts were at all times the work of one Person. Yet, those very acts which were performed by one Person are not confused, in our thinking, by any mixing of them; we decide from the character of the acts what is pertinent to each nature.

ST. BASIL:

Letters

After all these, in the last days, Christ Himself was manifested in the flesh, "born of a woman, born under the Law, that he might redeem those who were under the Law, that we might receive the adoption of sons." If, therefore, the sojourn of the Lord in the flesh had not taken place, there would have been no Redeemer to pay the price for us, nor Anyone to destroy the domination of death.

For, if that which is subject to death were one thing, and that which was assumed by the Lord were another, then death would not have ceased performing its own works, nor would the sufferings of the God-bearing flesh have become our gain. He would not have destroyed sin in the flesh. We who would die in Adam would not have been made to live in Christ. That which had fallen asunder would not have been restored; that which was shattered would not have been repaired; that which had been estranged through the deceit of the serpent would not have been made God's own.

For all these things are done away with by those who say that the Lord made His sojourn with a heavenly body. And what was the need of the

Excerpts from letter 261

94

blessed Virgin, if the God-bearing flesh was not to be assumed from the substance of Adam? But who is so bold as now to revive once more through sophistic words and the testimony, as they pretend, of the Scriptures, the teaching of Valentinus, which was disproved long ago?

This impiety of the "appearance", in fact, is not something new, but it was begun long ago by the weak-minded Valentinus who, taking a few detached phrases of the Apostle, constructed the impious fiction for himself, saying that He had taken on "the nature of a slave," and not the slave himself, and that the Lord had been made "in the form", but that humanity itself had not been assumed by Him. These men, whom we ought to deplore bitterly since they are bringing new disturbances with them, seem to be trying to revive an old heresy among you.

Now, as to their saying that human feelings pass over to the Godhead itself, that is characteristic of those who never preserve any consistency in thoughts and are unaware that some feelings are of the flesh and others of flesh endowed with a soul, and still others of a soul using a body. Now it is a property of flesh to be cut and lessened and destroyed, and again, of flesh endowed with a soul to suffer weariness and pain and hunger and thirst and to be overcome by sleep; and the properties of a soul using a body are griefs and anxieties and cares and all such things.

Some of these are natural and necessary to the living creatures, but some are due to a depraved will, brought on by a life that is dissolute and not trained to virtue. Therefore, it is evident that the Lord took on the natural feelings for a confirmation of the true Incarnation and not of one according to appearance, but rejected as unworthy of the undefiled Godhead the feelings arising from vice which soil the purity of our souls. For this reason it is said that He was "made in the likeness of sinful flesh."

Accordingly, He took our flesh with its natural feelings, but He "did no sin." Yet, even as death in the flesh, which was handed down to us through Adam, was swallowed up by the Godhead, so also sin was utterly destroyed by the justice which is in Jesus Christ, so that in the resurrection we resume our flesh, which is neither liable to death nor subject to sin.

These are, brethren, the mysteries of the Church; these are the traditions of the Fathers.

ST. JOHN DAMASCENE:

The Orthodox Faith

The things that are said about Christ fall into four general classes, for, while some apply to Him before the Incarnation, others do in the union, others after the union, and still others after the Resurrection.

Of those applying before the Incarnation, there are six kinds. Thus, some show the union of nature and consubstantiality with the Father, as "I and the Father are one"; "He that seeth me seeth the Father also"; "Who being in the form of God ... " and the like.

Others show the perfection of the hypostasis, as "Son of God"; "figure of His substance"; "Angel of great counsel, Wonderful, Counsellor," and the like.

Others show the mutual indwelling of the Persons in one another, as "I am in the Father and the Father in me," and their inseparable indwelling, as Word, Wisdom, Power, and Brightness. For the word, meaning the substantial word, while springing from the mind dwells in it inseparably from it; and also wisdom in the mind, the power in the strength, and the brightness in the light.

Excerpts from Book 4, chapter 18.

5. *Jesus Lord*

Others show how He is from the Father as from a cause, as "the Father is greater than I," for from Him He had His being and everything that He has—His being by generation, that is, not by creation; and as "I come forth from the Father and I am come," and "I live by the Father." Now everything that He has He has not by communication and not by instruction, but as from a cause, as "the Son cannot do anything of Himself, but that which He seeth the Father doing." The Son is from the Father, and in the Father and simultaneously with the Father, and not after Him. Similarly, also, what He does He does of Him, and with Him, for the will, operation and power of the Father and of the Son and of the Holy Spirit are identical—not like, but the same.

Others show how things willed by the Father are fulfilled by Him, not as by an instrument or a servant, but as by His substantial and subsistent Word, Wisdom and Power, because motion in Father and Son are seen to be one, as "all things were made by Him."

Some, finally, are said prophetically. Of these some are said as future, as, for example the words of Zacharias: "Behold thy King will come to thee." Others, however, refer to future events as past, as "This is our God ... afterwards He was seen upon earth and conversed with men."

There are three kinds of things said of Him in the union of the two natures in His one person. Thus when we talk from the point of view of the more excellent, we speak of "deification of the flesh," "becoming the Word," "exaltation" and the like, showing the wealth accrued to the flesh by its union and intimate conjunction with the sublime Divine Word. When on the other hand, we talk from the point of view of the less excellent, we speak of the "Incarnation" of God the Word, His "being made man," "emptying Himself," "poverty," "abasement," because these things and their like are attributed to God the Word on account of His being compounded with the humanity.

But, when we talk with both in mind, we speak of "union," "communication," "anointing," "conformation" and the like. Thus, by this third kind of things said, the first two already mentioned are implied, for by the union there is shown what each one had from the junction and mutual indwelling of the one co-existing with it.

Because of this hypostatic union the flesh is said to have been deified, to have become God and of the same divinity with the Word. At the same time, God the Word is said to have become flesh, to have become man, to be declared a creature.

There are three kinds of things said about Christ after the union. The first is indicative of the divine nature, as "I am in the Father and the Father in me," and "I and the Father are one." Then, everything that is attributed to Him before the union may also be attributed to Him after the union, with the exception of the fact that He has not yet assumed the flesh and its natural properties.

The second is indicative of the human nature, as "Why do you seek to kill me, a man who has spoken the truth to you," and "so must the Son of man be lifted up," and the like.

Now, there are six kinds of things that have been said and written about Christ the Savior in His human quality. Some are as natural as His birth and growth; His hunger, thirst, weariness, tears, sleeping, being pierced with nails, death, and all such other things as are natural and blameless passions. He might show that besides being God He was truly man. It is understood that these truly belong to His body and that the divinity suffered none of them, but through them worked our salvation. Other things He did in assuming a human way of acting, as, for example asking "Where have you laid Lazarus?"

Yet other things are said by appropriation and relatively, as "Him who knew no sin, he hath made sin for us," and "being made a curse for us." Others are by a distinction of reason. Thus, if you make distinction in your mind between things which are really inseparable, that is to say, between the flesh and the Word, then He is said to be a servant, and servile. In the same way, also, He called the Father His God.

Some things are said for our enlightenment and assurance, as "Glorify thou me, O Father, with thyself, with the glory which I had before the world was." Others are in accordance with His appropriation of the appearance of the Jews and His counting Himself as one of them, as when He said to the Samaritan woman: "You adore that which you know not; we adore that which we know. For salvation is of the Jews." The third kind of things said about Christ after the union is that which is indicative of the one Person and displays both natures, as for example: "I live by the Father: so he that eateth Me, the same shall also live by me"; and, "no man ascended into heaven, but He that descended from heaven, the Son of man who is in heaven," and the like.

And now, finally, some of the things which are said about Christ after the resurrection pertain to the divinity, as, "baptizing them in the name of the Father and of the Son and of the Holy Spirit"; and, "Behold I am with you all days, even to the consummation of the world," and the like. Some, however, pertain to the humanity, as, "they took hold of his feet," and the like. Others refer to both natures, as "I ascend to my Father and your Father, to my God and your God."

Therefore, we must attribute the sublime things to the divine nature, which is naturally superior to passions and the flesh, whereas we must attribute the lowly ones to the human nature. But those which are common to both we must attribute to the composite, that is to say to the one Christ who is God and man. And we must understand that both belong to one and the same, our Lord Jesus Christ. For, if we know what is proper to each and see that both are done by One, we shall believe rightly and not be deceived.

From all these things, the distinction between the united natures is known, as well as the fact that Cyril of Alexandria says, although the divinity and humanity are not identical in their natural quality, there is definitely one Son and Christ and Lord. And since He is one, then His Person is also one, and no division whatsoever will be introduced into the hypostatic union by our recognition of the difference between the natures.

ST. BERNARD:

On the Circumcision

O truly wonderful mystery! The boy is circumcised and named Jesus. How are these things connected? You would think that circumcision is for those in need of salvation, not for the Savior. You would think it preferable for Him to perform the work of salvation, rather than be the subject of it.

Yet, see how this Mediator between God and man, from the very first instant of His birth joins the divine and the human, the highest and the lowest. He is born of a woman, but in such a way that the flower of her virginity is not harmed in any way by her motherhood.

He is wrapped in swaddling clothes, but even in this humble garb He is praised by angelic choirs; He is tucked away in a manger, but a radiant star keeps watch.

The circumcision proves, beyond a shadow of doubt, the fact of His humanity; the name indicates the majesty of His glory. He was circumcised because He was truly a son of Abraham; He was called Jesus, the Name that is above all names, because He was truly the Son of God.

Excerpts from the first sermon on the Circumcision of the Lord

Unlike those before Him who had the same name as a mere title, Jesus bears His name as the truth which before had only been symbolized. Heaven itself had given Him this name, for the Evangelist says it is the name "which was used by the angel just before He was conceived in the womb."

Note the depth of this thought. He is called Jesus after His birth by men, but the angel acknowledged this even before His conception. He is the Savior of both angels and men; of men by reason of the Incarnation; of angels, from the time of their creation.

"The name given Him," writes St. Luke, "was Jesus, which was used by the angel." A deed is proven by the word of two or three witnesses. What had been symbolized by the prophets is now made manifest by the Gospels—the Savior is Incarnate. Although the Christ does not need witnesses, either angelic or human, yet for the sake of the elect, these are called. Chief among the witnesses are three—the angel, the Virgin Mother, and the virtuous Joseph.

Of this Child it had been written: "From the top of His head to the very soles of His feet, there is no beauty left." That He submitted to the knife eight days after His birth was merely to point toward the crucifixion which, thirty years later, would be the complete fulfillment of the prophecy.

We, too, brethren, must be circumcised if we are to be worthy of the name of our Savior. No longer is it necessary that we be circumcised in the flesh for the cleansing of one member of the body. We must be circumcised in spirit and truth for the cleansing of the whole body. The cleansing of the whole man is effected in Baptism; then it is necessary that we grow as men, in virtue, to full perfection.

Christ gave us the example of virtue in action, particularly humility and obedience. Christ had no need of circumcision, since it was impossible that He commit or inherit sin. As He grew to manhood, it was evident that He neither could nor did commit sin. It is even more evident that He could not contract sin from His eternal Father, or His most pure Mother. Yet the Boy was circumcised, a most pure Lamb, without spot. We must blush, indeed, if we do not learn from such example!

Chapter 4

THE

WONDROUS

WORKS

OF

GOD

O Lord, our Lord, how admirable
is Thy name in the whole earth;
For Thy magnificence is elevated
above the heavens.

Psalm 8:1

*How many men, lame and crippled and blind, left Christ after
a cure, glorying in their new power and praising the wonderful
works of God! How often the crowd dispersed at night glorifying
God "because He had given such power to men!" Never did a
man perform such deeds or teach such lessons.*

Indeed, one of the most marvellous of the works of Our Lord was His teaching mission among men. It is easy to be lost in wonder over His miracles but we must never forget that He came to save us, to lead us to God. It is really a joy to celebrate the liturgy of the great mysteries of His life at Christmas, Easter, and Pentecost and to draw lessons from them. But between these "high spots" in the Gospels, the good news of Christ's teachings are a wondrous work, given for our spiritual growth.

Our jaded modern world is enjoying greater material wealth than has ever been known to history. Grateful as we must be to God for these temporal gifts, there is the attendant danger of mistaking these material things for an end, rather than a means. Christ's insistent call to charity and justice can be drowned out by the clamorous charm of materialism.

Civil rights and social justice are simply modern day applications of the priceless truths that Our Lord taught, day in and day out, during His public life. Christ suffers again in the poor of Africa and Asia, the naked and hungry of Latin America. He still suffers His agony with the oppressed Negro; His passion continues in the outcast Puerto Rican or Mexican. His condemnation of the Pharisees continues for those who refuse just wages to their workers or decent family living conditions. Wherever bigotry, prejudice or anti-Semitism still flourish, Christ is crucified over and over again!

Our Lord is ever the Good Shepherd, tenderly nourishing His flock, and vitally interested in all that concerns it.

CLEMENT OF ALEXANDRIA:

Christ the Educator

The nature of His love for men and of His method of educating His little ones we have described as far as lay in our power. He pictures His teaching cogently, by likening it to a "grain of mustard seed." With such a figure, He depicts the spiritual nature of the word that is sown, the productiveness it has by nature, and the growth and the greatness latent in the power of the word. By the bitterness of the mustard seed he suggests, too, that the unpleasantness and purgative nature of correction are all to our advantage. At any rate, through this allegory of the small mustard seed, applicable in so many ways, He proves that He bestows salvation on all mankind.

Of old, the Word educated through Moses, and after that through the Prophets; even Moses was, in fact, a Prophet. For the Law was the education of children difficult to control. "Having eaten their fill," Scriptures says, "they got up to play." And since they were continually filling themselves without obeying reason, and playing without listening

Excerpts from Book 1, chapters 11 and 12

to reason, the Law and fear followed them to restrain them from sin, and to encourage them to reform themselves.

So it disposed them to give ready obedience to the true Educator; then the one same Word directed their docility toward what was of obligation. "The law has been given," Paul says, "as our educator in Christ." Then it is obvious that the one person who is alone reliable, just, good, Jesus, the Son of the Father as His image and likeness, the Word of God, is our Educator. It is to Him that God has entrusted us, as a loving Father delivering His children to a true Educator, for as He expressly commanded us: "This is my beloved Son: hear Him."

Our divine Educator is trustworthy, for He is endowed with three excellent qualities: intelligence, good will and the authority to speak. With intelligence, because He is the Wisdom of the Father: "All wisdom is from the Lord and hath always been with Him." With authority to speak, because He is God and Creator: "All things were made through Him, and without Him was made nothing." With good will, because He is the only one who has given Himself as a sacrifice for us: "The good shepherd lays down His life for His sheep," and in fact He did lay it down. Surely, good will is nothing else than willing what is good for the neighbor for his own sake.

From the subjects we have already discussed it must be concluded that Jesus, our Educator, has outlined for us the true life, and that He educates the man who abides in Him. His character is not excessively fear-inspiring, yet neither is it over-indulgent in its kindness. He imposes commands, but at the same time expresses them in such a way that we can fulfill them.

It seems to me that the reason He formed man from dust, gave him a second birth through water, increase through the Spirit, education by the Word, thereby guiding him surely to the adoption of sons and to salvation with holy precepts, was precisely that He might transform an earth-born man into a holy and heavenly creature by His coming, and accomplish the original divine command: "Let us make mankind in our image and likeness." It is Christ, in fact, who is, in all its perfection, what God then commanded; others are so only by a certain image.

As for us, O children of a good Father, flock of a good Educator, let us fulfill the will of the Father, let us obey the Word, and let us be truly molded by the saving life of the Savior. Then, since we shall already be living the life of heaven which makes us divine, let us anoint ourselves with the never-failing oil of gladness, the incorruptible oil of sweet odor. We possess an unmistakable model of incorruptibility in the life of our Lord and are following in the footsteps of God.

His main concern is to consider the ways and means by which the life of man might be made more conformable to salvation. He does truly make this His concern. He seeks to train us to the condition of a wayfarer, that is, to make us well-girded and unimpeded, that we might be self-sufficient of life and practice a moderate frugality in our journey toward the good life of eternity, telling us that each one of us is to be his own storehouse: "Do not be anxious about tomorrow." He means to say that each one who has dedicated himself to Christ ought to be self-sufficient and his own servant and, besides, live his life from day to day.

We are educated not for war but for peace. In war there is need for much equipment, just as self-indulgence craves abundance. But peace and love, simple and plain blood sisters, do not need arms nor abundant supplies. Their nourishment is the Word, the Word whose leadership enlightens and educates, from whom we learn poverty and humility and all that goes with love of freedom and of mankind and of the good. Simply, through Him we become like God by a likeness of virtue. Labor, then, and do not grow weary; you will become what you dare not hope or cannot imagine.

As there is one sort of training for philosophers, another for orators and another for wrestlers, so too, there is an excellent disposition imparted by the education of Christ that is proper to the free will loving the good. As for deeds, walking and reclining at table, eating and sleeping, marriage relations and the manner of life, the whole of a man's education all become illustrious as holy deeds under the influence of the Educator. The education Christ gives is in harmony with man's nature.

That is why the Word is called Savior, because He has left men remedies of reason to effect understanding and salvation, and because, awaiting the favorable opportunity, He corrects evil, diagnoses the cause of passion, extracts the roots of unreasonable lusts, advises what we should avoid, and applies all the remedies of salvation to those who are sick.

This is the greatest and most noble of all God's acts: saving mankind. But those who labor under some sickness are dissatisfied if the physician prescribes no remedy to restore their health. How, then, can we withhold our sincerest gratitude from the Divine Teacher when He corrects the acts of disobedience that sweep us on to ruin and uproots the desires that drag us into sin, refusing to be silent and connive at them, and even offers counsels on the right way to live? Certainly we owe Him the deepest gratitude.

Do we say, then, that the rational animal, I mean man, ought to do anything else besides contemplate the divinity? I maintain that he ought to contemplate human nature, also, and live as the truth leads him, admiring the way in which the Educator and His precepts are worthy of one another and adapted one to the other. In keeping with such a model, we ought also to adapt ourselves to our Educator, conform our deeds to the Word, and then we will truly live.

ST. AMBROSE:

Second Oration on Faith in the Resurrection

The Lord shows in the gospel, to come to specific instances, how a person will rise again. He not only quickened Lazarus, He quickened the faith of all. For, when the Lord went to the sepulchre and loudly cried out: "Lazarus, come forth," what other meaning is there in this except that He wished to give visible proof, to exemplify our future resurrection.

Why did He cry out loudly? Was it because He was not used to working through the Spirit, or because He was not wont to command in silence? No, He intended rather to emphasize the Scriptural statement "that in a moment, in the twinkling of an eye, at the last trumpet, the dead shall rise again incorruptible." For the lifting of His voice corresponds to the peal of trumpets. When He cried out: "Lazarus come forth," why did He add the specific name, except, perhaps, lest one might be raised instead of another, or lest the resurrection might seem accidental rather than something commanded?

The dead man, therefore, heard and came forth from the tomb. He was bound hand and foot

Excerpts from section 77 ff.

with bandages, and his face was covered with a cloth. Imagine, if you can, how he picks his way with eyes closed, moves forward with his feet tied, and makes progress without taking separate steps. Although the bands remained, they did not hold him back. Although his eyes were covered, they saw. Accordingly, he who arose walked, and left his sepulchre, and had sight. For, where the power of a divine command was operating, nature had no need of its own functions, and, as if in a kind of trance, no longer followed its own course, but obeyed the divine will. The bonds of death were broken before those of the tomb.

If anyone is astonished at this, let him inquire who gave the command and his astonishment will cease. It was Jesus Christ, the Power of God, the Life, the Light, the Resurrection of the dead. The Power lifted up a man lying in the grave; the Life made him walk; the Light dispelled the darkness and restored his sight; the Resurrection renewed the gift of life.

In order that they who refused to believe in their hearts might at least believe their eyes, they removed the stone, they saw the corpse, they smelled the stench, they broke the bands. They could not deny that he was dead whom they saw rising again. They saw the marks of death and the proofs of life. What wonder if, as they worked, they had a change of heart in the process, and, as they heard, they at least believed their ears! What wonder if, as they looked, they were forced to believe their eyes, and, as they broke the bonds, they loosened the shackles of their minds! What wonder if, as Lazarus was being unbound, the people were set free, and, as they allowed him to go off, they themselves returned to God! Therefore, many who had come to Mary, seeing what was done, believed.

Nor was this the only instance our Lord Jesus Christ afforded us, but He raised others, also, that we might believe at least on the basis of more numerous examples. Moved by the tears of a widowed mother, He raised up a young man. Approaching and touching the stretcher, He said, "Young man, I say to thee, arise. And he who was dead, sat up, and began to speak." The moment he heard, he sat up and spoke. The gift of power, then, is one thing, and the order of human nature another.

And what shall I say about the daughter of the ruler of the synagogue, at whose death the people were mourning and the flute players were playing their music? In the belief that she was indeed dead, solemn funeral services were being performed. The spirit returned immediately at the voice of the Lord. She arose with revived body, and she partook of food to furnish proof that she was alive.

And why should we wonder that a soul is restored at the word of God, and flesh returns to bones, when we recall that a dead person was restored to life by physical contact with the body of a Prophet? Elias prayed and restored a dead child to life. Peter, in the name of Christ, bade Tabitha rise and walk. The poor rejoiced that she was restored to them and believed on account of the food she gave them.

Shall we not believe, at the risk of our salvation? They purchased the resurrection of another by their tears. Shall we doubt that ours was purchased by the Passion of Christ? When He gave up His spirit to show that He had died for our resurrection, He exemplified the course of the resurrection itself. For, as soon as He again cried out with a loud voice and gave up His spirit, the earth quaked, and the rocks were rent, and the tombs were opened, and many bodies of the saints who had fallen asleep arose, and, coming forth out of the tombs after His Resurrection, they came into the holy city and appeared to many.

If these things occurred when He gave up His spirit, why should we think it incredible when He returns for judgment, especially since this earlier resurrection is a proof of that future resurrection, a pattern of the reality to come? Indeed, it is less a pattern than it is the truth itself. Who, then, at our Lord's Passion, opened the graves and assisted the dead to rise and showed them how to find their way to the holy city? If there was no one, it was certainly Divine Power working in the bodies of the dead. Does one seek human aid when he clearly sees the work of God?

God has no need of human assistance. God commanded the heavens to come into existence, and it was done. He decided to create the earth, and it was created. Who carried the stones upon his shoulders? Who paid the cost? Who helped Him at the work? These things were done in a moment. Do you want to know how quickly? "He spoke and they were made."

If the material universe sprang into being at a word, why should not the dead also rise again at a word? Although they were dead, yet they once were alive, they had the sense of feeling and knowing, and they had the power of acting. Furthermore, there is the greatest difference between not being capable of life and remaining lifeless. The devil said, "Command this stone to become a loaf of bread." When he confesses that, at God's command, material nature can be transformed, do you not clearly see that, at God's command, nature can be made anew?

ST. BASIL:

Letters

Let us first propose these words: "I live because of the Father." In this place the expression does not refer to His life before time—for nothing which has life because of something else can be self-existent; just as nothing that is heated by something else can be heat itself; and our Christ and God has said: "I am the life." But the life which He had because of the Father is this life which He has had in the flesh and here in time.

And again, consider the words: "My Father is greater than I." I am convinced that by this expression the Son of God is proved consubstantial with the Father, since I know that comparisons hold good only in the case of things of the same nature. For, we say that one angel is greater than another angel, and one man is more just than another man, and one bird is swifter than another bird. If, therefore, comparisons are made of objects of the same species, and, the Father, by comparison, is said to be greater than the Son, the Son is consubstantial with the Father.

But there is also another thought contained in this saying. Nay, what wonder is it if He confessed that the Father was greater than He Himself, since,

Excerpts from the eighth letter.

being the Word and having been made flesh, He seemed less than the angels in glory and less than man in appearance. For it is said, "Thou hast made him a little less than the angels," and, "We have seen him and there was no comeliness nor beauty, but his appearance was the most abject of all men." He endured all these things because of His great love for His creatures, that He might rescue the lost sheep and, having saved it, brought it back.

And will those who would deny Christ's full divinity make the manger a subject of reproach to Him, the manger in which, while a helpless infant, He was nurtured by the Word? And will He be taunted because of His poverty, because He, the reputed son of a carpenter, was not provided with a cradle? In this way the Son is less than the Father, because for your sake He died in order that He might free us from death and cause us to share in the heavenly life.

For our sake, too, He does not know the hour or the day of judgment; yet nothing is unknown to true Wisdom, for through Him are all things made. Moreover, among men no one is ignorant of what he has made. But He so provides for our weakness, lest sinners, by reason of the brief time allotted them, fall into despair, believing that no time is left them for repentance; and again, lest those fighting a long battle against the opposing force, because of its protracted duration, should desert their posts. Therefore, He provides for both by assuming ignorance.

Only that Father, He says, knows, since He Himself is the end and final beatitude. For when we learn to know God no longer in a mirror, nor through an alien medium, but when we approach Him as the Only and the One, then we shall also know the final beatitude. But our dulled intellect is bound up with material and mixed with clay, and so is unable to be intent on pure contemplation.

We apprehend the activities of the Creator only by being led through the beauties akin to our own body, and meanwhile, we learn to know these things from their effects, so that, strengthened little by little, we may at some time be able to approach the unveiled Divinity Itself. It is with this meaning, I think, that the following words were spoken: "My Father is greater than I," and, "That is not mine to give you, but it belongs to those for whom it has been prepared by my Father." For, this is also the meaning of Christ handing over the kingdom to God and the Father, since He is the first-fruits and not the end according, as I have said, to the empirical knowledge, which looks to us and not to the Son Himself.

Again, according to the words of the wise Solomon in the Proverbs, He, the Uncreated, was

121

created. "For the Lord," he says, "created me." And He is called, "the beginning of the evangelical ways" which lead us to the kingdom of heaven, since He is not a creature in substance, but was made the "way" in the divine dispensation. For, being "made" and "created" have the same meaning. In fact, as He was made a way, so also was He made a door, a shepherd, a messenger, a sheep, and, in turn, a high priest and apostle, different names being given according to the different conceptions.

And, what can be said concerning the unsubjected God and One who was made "sin" for our sakes? For it is written, "And when all things are made subject to him, then the Son himself will also be made subject to him who subjected all things to him." Do you not fear, O man, the God who is called unsubjected? For He makes your subjection His own, and, because of your struggle against virtue, He calls Himself unsubjected. Thus He even says at one time that He Himself was the One persecuted; for He says: "Saul, Saul, why dost thou persecute me?" when Saul was hastening to Damascus, desiring to put in bonds the disciples of Christ.

Again, He calls Himself naked if anyone of His brethren is naked. "I was naked," He says, "and you covered me." And still again, when another was in prison, He said that He Himself was the One imprisoned. For He Himself took up our infirmities and bore the burden of our ills. And one of our infirmities is insubordination, and this He bore. Therefore, even the adversities which happen to us the Lord makes His own, taking upon Himself our sufferings because of His fellowship with us.

ST. CYPRIAN:

The Good of Patience

And in order that we may be able to understand more fully, beloved brethren, that patience is an attribute of God and that whoever is gentle, patient and meek is an imitator of God the Father, when in His gospel the Lord was giving salutary precepts and in revealing the divine counsels was instructing His disciples unto perfection, He made this pronouncement: "You have heard that it was said, 'Thou shalt love thy neighbor and shalt hate thy enemy.' But I say to you, love your enemies and pray for those who persecute you, so that you may be children of your Father in heaven, who makes His sun to rise on the good and the evil, and sends rain on the just and the unjust.

"For if you love those who love you, what reward shall you have? Do not even the publicans do this? And if you salute your brethren only, what are you doing more than others? Do not even the gentiles do that? You, therefore, will be perfect as your heavenly Father is perfect."

He said that it is in this way that the sons of God are made perfect. He showed that it is in this way that we attain our goal, and He taught that we

Excerpts from chapters 5, 6, 7

are restored by a heavenly birth, if the patience of God the Father abide in us, if the divine likeness which Adam lost by sin be manifested and shine in our actions. What glory it is to become like God! What wonderful and what great happiness it is to possess among our virtues what can be put on a par with the divine merits!

And this, beloved brethren, Jesus Christ, our Lord and our God, did not teach by words only, but He also fulfilled it by His deeds. And He who said that He came down for this purpose, namely to do the will of His Father, among the other miracles of virtue by which He gave proof of His divine majesty, also preserved and exemplified His Father's patience by His habitual forbearance.

Accordingly, His every act right from the very outset of His coming is marked by an accompanying patience. From the first moment of His descent from the sublimity of heavenly to earthly things, He did not disdain, though the Son of God, to put on man's flesh, and although He Himself was not a sinner, to bear the sins of others. Having put aside His immortality for a time, He suffered Himself to become mortal, in order that, though innocent, He might be slain for the salvation of the guilty.

The Lord was baptized by His servant, and He, although destined to grant the remission of sins, did not Himself disdain to have His body cleansed with water of regeneration. He, through whom others are fed, fasted for forty days. He felt hunger and starvation so that those who were famished for the Word of God and grace might be filled with the Bread of Heaven. He engaged in conflict with the devil who tempted Him, and content with having vanquished so formidable an enemy, He did not carry the fight beyond words.

He did not rule His disciples as a master rules his slaves, but being both kind and gentle, He loved them as a brother, even deigning to wash the feet of His apostles, that He might teach by His example. We should not wonder, then, that He was such a, one among His disciples, who was able to tolerate Judas, even to the end, with enduring patience.

But what wonderful equanimity in bearing with the Jewish officials, and what wonderful patience in persuading the unbelieving to accept the faith, in winning the ungrateful by kindness, in responding gently to those who contradicted Him, in enduring the proud with mercy, in yielding with humility to persecutors, in wishing to win over those who persistently rebelled against God—even to the very hour of His passion and death!

But in that very hour of His passion and cross, before they had come to the cruel act of His slaughter and the shedding of His blood, what violent abuses He listened to with patience, and what shame-

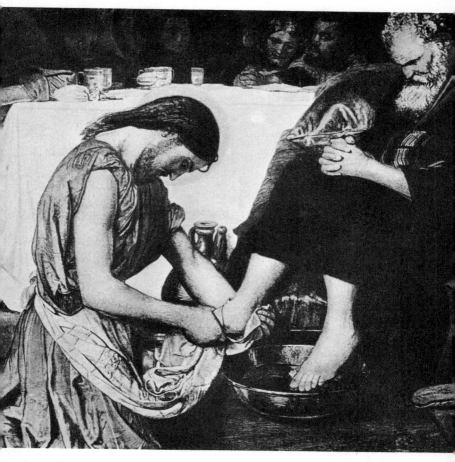

Jesus Washes the Apostles' Feet, FORD MADOX BROWN
National Gallery, London

"He did not rule His disciples as a master rules his slaves,
but being both kind and gentle, He loved them as a brother,
even deigning to wash the feet of His apostles, that He
might teach by His example."

ST. CYPRIAN

ful insults He endured! He was even covered with the spittle of His revilers, when, but a short time before, with His own spittle, He had cured the eyes of the blind man.

He who now crowns the martyrs with eternal garlands was Himself crowned with thorns. He who clothes all others with the garment of immortality was stripped of His earthly garment. He who has offered us the cup of salvation was given vinegar to drink. He the innocent, He the just, He who is Innocence itself and Justice itself, is counted among the criminals.

The Word of God, silent, is led to the cross. And although the stars are confounded at the crucifixion of the Lord, the elements are disturbed, the earth trembles, night blots out the day, the sun withdraws its rays and its eyes lest it be forced to gaze upon this crime, yet He does not speak, nor is He moved, nor does He proclaim His majesty, even during the suffering itself. He endures all things, even to the end, with a constant perseverance so that in Christ a full and perfect patience may find its realization.

ST. VALERIAN:

On Mercy

Dearly beloved, if you look back over all the stages of justice through which the work of religion is carried on, you will not find anyone who gives a gracious service to the Lord and through it fails to win a place of dignity with Him.

But although these very acts which faith works in us do proceed from human endeavor, they should be ascribed to God. If there are any deeds well done, it is through Him and in Him that they have existence, and are stored up for the future as profitable to individual men.

Wherefore, let no one who is wise think that the benefits of God should be ascribed to his own powers. Otherwise, he will hear that phrase of the Apostle which says: "What hast thou that thou hast not received? Or if thou hast received it, why dost thou boast as if thou hadst not received it?"

Dearly beloved, we are well aware that, according to the Gospel doctrine which recounts the promises of beatitude, justice has prepared a place for man in heaven. Purity of heart has merited to see Christ. Mercy has received a similar reward

Excerpts from the seventh homily

of retribution. The joy of peace has prepared for many a place among the children of God. The sufferings of the saints have gained the crown of victory and the glory of the celestial kingdom because of the merits of their virtue.

But, one and the same power of the Father, Son and the Holy Spirit works all these things in us. It gives a perfection to our works of righteousness, and supplies to a good will whatever best aids there are. There is, indeed, one thing, and that very great, which descends from the abode of mercy. In it a mortal man can justly claim glory for himself. It is to feed the poor and to redeem the captives—if, however, neither boastfulness dissipates this glory or unpleasant sadness throws it into disorder.

Behold, you hear the Evangelist saying, "Come, blessed of my Father, take possession with me of the kingdom prepared for you from the foundation of the world; for I was hungry and you gave me to eat; I was thirsty and you gave me to drink; naked and you covered me." Therefore, as you perceive, if it becomes anyone to glory, he should not do it except because of this activity, by which the Lord orders that He Himself be fed and clothed, and that His hunger be satisfied day by day with a little portion of divided bread.

Wherefore, if we desire our glorying not to be vain, let us in the first place redeem the friendship of the highest King by our copious alms. To open the heavenly kingdom to ourselves, let us all turn our attention to showing mercy to the Lord. In this love of Him, we should not regard the tears of the poor lightly or negligently, lest, to our confusion, He who feeds all the world may be seen hungry among those who are begging. Gaze upon the needs of every one of these, and on our Savior's concern for the wretched. You will understand that our Christ is present wherever you behold an abundance of tears.

You do not have to seek the Lord far away, if you are not a miser. Look, He awaits us right outside with that crowd of His servants. You do not have to cast your glance now here, now there, so that you doubt whom to make the chief beneficiary of your pitiful expenditure. Know that our Christ is that man whom you see naked, whom you see as a blind man, whom you meet in a lame man, whom you behold wrapped in rags or covered with dirty garments.

In this clothing, indeed, was He found when sought by the Magi. Dressed like this and lying in the manger was He when He received the gifts they offered from their open treasures. That Gospel phrase has a bearing on these matters which says: "Lay up for yourselves treasures in heaven where neither rust consumes nor thieves break in." These are those treasures which are recorded among our merits stored up in heaven, treasures which nothing adverse spoils. That is the significance of dividing the substance of our resources among the poor.

There are, indeed, many degrees of mercy, but we should inquire what the chief ones are. The first kind of mercy is, in truth, to extend a helping hand to a fallen man, to show the way of salvation to the wanderer, to visit the sick, perseveringly to console those who are tried by tribulation. Yet, this is the mercy we should especially long for: to feed the hungry, to clothe the naked, to ransom the captive, to make a loan for a time to one who needs it.

Dearly beloved, what more do you seek in return for disbursing a bit of divided bread? Even if a share in the heavenly kingdom had not been promised you for it, as sinners you ought to be content with that statement which has brought to mortal man the hope of future salvation and the joy of everlasting security. For, if consideration is given to the fruits of your work and the tenderness of heavenly love, you receive far more than you give.

Look, in return for feeding a poor man, the Gospels promise you the kingdom of heaven. Because of your dividing and sharing your bread, or offering hospitable shelter, or clothing the naked, the Lord promises you, through the Prophets, His help when you invoke Him. As the Psalms tell, the justice arising from your mercy is stored up forever and ever.

If we compare heavenly things with earthly, it is evident that something very valuable is for sale at a very low price. How great is your alms in proportion to all the things which the Lord has clearly promised to mortal men? Look, we give earthly goods; He, those of heaven. We offer goods which last for a while; He, those which endure forever.

ST. BASIL:

Homily on Psalm 33

"This poor man cried, and the Lord heard him."
Ps. 33:7.

Poverty is not always praiseworthy, but only
that which is practiced intentionally, according to
the evangelical aim. Many are poor in their resources, but very grasping in their intention. Poverty does not save these; on the contrary, their intention condemns them. Accordingly, not he who is
poor is by all means blessed, but he who has considered the command of Christ better than the
treasures of the world.

These the Lord also pronounces blessed when
He says, "Blessed are the poor in spirit," not those
poor in resources, but those who from their souls
have chosen poverty. For, nothing that is not delib-
erate is to be pronounced blessed. Therefore, every
virtue, but this one especially before all others, is
characterized by the action of the free will.

So it is said, "This poor man cried." By the de-
monstrative word for the man who was poor because of God, and hungry and thirsty and naked, he
calls forth your understanding: "This poor man,"

Excerpts from section 5, 6, 10

134

all but pointing with his finger; this disciple of Christ. It is possible also to refer this expression to Christ, who being rich by nature, because all things belonging to the Father are His, became poor for our sakes in order that by His poverty we might become rich.

Nearly every work that leads to the blessing, the Lord Himself began, setting Himself forth as an example to His disciples. Return to the blessings and you will find on examining each that He anticipated the teaching contained in the words by His deeds.

"Blessed are the meek." How, then, shall we learn meekness? "Learn from me, for I am meek and humble of heart." "Blessed are the peacemakers." Who will teach us the beauty of peace? The Peacemaker Himself, who made peaceful by the blood of His cross both things of heaven and those of earth. "Blessed are the poor." He Himself is the one who was poor and who emptied Himself in the form of a slave in order that "Of His fullness we might all receive, grace for grace."

"O taste and see that the Lord is sweet." Ps. 33:9.

Frequently we have noticed that the faculties of the soul are called by the same name as external members. Since our Lord is true Bread and His flesh true Meat, it is necessary that the pleasure of enjoyment of the Bread be in us through a spiritual taste. As the nature of honey can be described to the inexperienced not so much by speech as by the perception of it through taste, so the goodness of the heavenly Word cannot be clearly taught by doctrines, unless, examining to a greater extent the dogmas of truth, we are able to comprehend by our own experience the goodness of the Lord.

"Taste," he said, but not "be filled," because now we know in part and through a mirror and in an obscure manner we see the truth; but the time will come when the present pledge and this taste of grace will attain to the perfection of enjoyment for us. Therefore, he says, "Taste," in order that you, hungering and thirsting after justice, may always be blessed: "Blessed is the man that hopeth in him." He who always has a desire for the Word will put his hope in nothing else than the Lord.

"Turn away from evil and do good, seek after peace and pursue it." Ps. 33:15.

Concerning this peace the Lord has said, "Peace I leave with you, my peace I give to you; not as the world gives peace do I give to you." Seek, therefore, after the peace of the Lord and pursue it. And you will not pursue it otherwise than by running toward the goal, to the prize of the heavenly calling. For, the true peace is from above.

Yet, as long as we are bound to the flesh, we are yoked to many things which also trouble us. Seek, then, after a peace, a release from the troubles of this world; possess a calm mind, a tranquil and unconfused state of soul, which is neither agitated by the passions nor drawn aside by false doctrines that challenge by their persuasiveness to assent, in order that you may obtain "the peace of God which surpasses all understanding and guards your heart."

He who seeks after peace seeks Christ, because "He Himself is our peace," who has made us into the new man, making peace, and "making peace through the blood of His cross, whether on earth or in the heavens."

ST. AUGUSTINE:

Sermon on the Mount

What therefore does He say? "Blessed are the poor in spirit, for theirs is the kingdom of heaven." Concerning the striving after temporal things we read what is written: "All is vanity and presumption of spirit." Now, presumption of spirit means arrogance and pride. And who does not know that the proud are said to be puffed up, as if bloated with wind? Hence, also, that saying of the Apostle: "Knowledge puffs up, but charity edifies."

Here, then, the poor in spirit are rightly understood as the humble and God-fearing—that is to say, those who do not have a puffed-up spirit, bloated with intellectual pride. And it would be entirely unfitting for blessedness to take its beginning from any other source, since it is to reach the summit of wisdom, for "the beginning of wisdom is fear of the Lord," and on the other hand pride is described as "the beginning of all sin." Let the proud, therefore, strive after the kingdoms of earth, and love them. But, "Blessed are the poor in spirit, for theirs is the kingdom of heaven."

"Blessed are the meek, for they shall inherit the land. This, I believe, is the land of which it is said in

Excerpts from Book 1

the Psalm: "Thou art my hope, my portion in the land of the living." For it denotes a certain firmness and stability of a perpetual inheritance, where, through its love of the good, the soul finds rest as in its proper place, just as the body finds rest on the land; where the soul is nourished by its proper food, just as the body is nourished from the land. For the saints this is, indeed, life and rest. The meek are those who submit to iniquities and do not resist evil, but overcome evil with good. Let the haughty, therefore, quarrel and contend for earthly and temporal things. But, "Blessed are the meek, for they shall inherit the land"—the land from which they cannot be expelled.

"Blessed are they that mourn, for they shall be comforted." Mourning is grief over the loss of things that are highly prized. Those who have been converted to God are losing the things which in this world they used to embrace as precious things, for they find no delight in the things which they used to enjoy. They are torn with grief until a love for eternal things is begotten in them. They shall be comforted, therefore, by the Holy Spirit—who on this account especially is called the Paraclete, that is, the Comforter—so that, when they have lost temporal happiness, they may fully enjoy the eternal.

"Blessed are they who hunger and thirst for justice, for they shall be satisfied." He calls them lovers of the true and unchangeable goodness. Therefore, they shall be satisfied with that food of which the Lord Himself says: "My food is to do the will of my Father,"—and this is justice. And they shall be satisfied with that water, of which, as the same Lord says: "Whosoever shall drink, it shall become in him a fountain of water springing up unto life everlasting."

"Blessed are the merciful, for they shall obtain mercy." He calls those blessed who come to the aid of the miserable, because their reward is so great that they shall be freed from misery.

"Blessed are the pure of heart, for they shall see God." How foolish, then, are those who try to find God through the use of bodily eyes! It is through the heart that God is seen, and in another passage it is written, "Seek Him in simplicity of heart." A simple heart is a heart that is pure; and just as light which surrounds us cannot be seen except through eyes that are clear, so neither is God seen unless that through which He can be seen is pure.

"Blessed are the peacemakers, for they shall be called the children of God." Where there is no contention, there is perfect peace. And because nothing can contend against God, the children of God are peacemakers; for, of course, children ought to have a likeness to their father. And those who calm their passions and subject them to reason, that is, subject them to mind and spirit, and who keep their carnal lusts under control—those engender peace within themselves and become a kingdom of God. They become a kingdom in which all things are so well ordered that everything in man which is common to us and to the beasts is spontaneously governed by that which is chief and pre-eminent in man, namely, reason and mind; and that this same pre-eminent faculty of man is itself subject to a still higher power, which is truth itself, the Only-begotten Son of God.

Man is unable to rule over the lower things unless he in turn submits to the rule of a higher being. And this is the peace which is promised "on earth to men of good will." This is the life of a man of consummate and perfect wisdom. The prince of this world, who rules over the perverse and disorderly, has been cast out of a thoroughly pacified and orderly kingdom of this kind. When this man has been established and strengthened in this peace, then he who has been cast out—no matter what persecutions he may stir up from without—increases the glory which is according to God. He does not weaken anything in the edifice, but, by the fact that his devices are of no avail, he makes known what great internal stability has been established. Therefore the next is "Blessed are they who suffer persecution for justice' sake, for theirs is the kingdom of heaven."

Each of these eight pronouncements is a maxim of universal application, hence each is worthy of careful consideration. The first mentioned source of blessedness is humility: "Blessed are the poor in spirit;" that is to say: Blessed are those who are not puffed up while the soul is submitting to divine authority, fearful that it may be on the way to punishments after this life, even though it may deem itself blessed in this life.

Now the soul takes up the study of the divine Scriptures. Here it must act with the meekness of piety, lest it become so bold as to censure whatever seems absurd to the uninstructed, and become indocile through obstinacy in disputing. From this study it begins to see by what worldly fetters it is being held because of sins and the way of the flesh. In this third stage there is understanding; therefore, there is mourning, since the supreme good is being lost when there is a clinging to lower goods.

In the fourth maxim there is labor, because the mind is eagerly striving to extricate itself from the things in which it is entangled by harmful pleasures; great fortitude is needed, because whatever is possessed with sinful delight is not relinquished without sorrow. But in the fifth stage a means of escape is offered to those who are persevering in labor; no one can escape these entanglements unless aided by a more powerful one. Therefore, blessed, indeed, are the merciful, for they shall obtain mercy.

In the sixth maxim there is purity of heart; by a blessed consciousness of good deeds the pure heart is able to contemplate the supreme good which cannot be discerned except by a pure and serene intellect. Finally, the seventh maxim is wisdom itself; it is the contemplation of truth, making the whole man peaceful, and taking on the likeness of God. It is summed up this way: "Blessed are the peacemakers, for they shall be called the children of God."

The eighth maxim returns, as it were, to the first; it presents and approves something consummate and perfect. Thus, the kingdom of heaven is named in the first stage and in the eighth. In the first, "Blessed are the poor in spirit, for theirs is the kingdom of heaven." And as though in answer to the question: "Who shall separate us from the love of Christ? Shall tribulation, or distress, or persecution, or hunger, or nakedness, or danger, or the sword,"—as though in answer, He says, "Blessed are they who suffer persecution for justice' sake, for theirs is the kingdom of heaven.

Therefore, there are seven maxims which constitute perfection, for the eighth starts anew, as it were, from the beginning: it clarifies and approves what is already complete. Thus, all the other grades of perfection are accomplished through these seven. It seems to me, then, that the sevenfold operation of the Holy Spirit coincides with these stages and maxims.

The Names and Titles of Our Savior

In the Holy Scriptures there are many names and titles which are applied to Our Lord and Savior, Jesus. He is said to be the Word; He is called Wisdom, Light and Power; right hand, arm and angel; man and lamb, sheep and priest. He is the Way, the Truth, the Life; a vine, Justice and Redemption; bread, a stone and doctor; a fount of living water, peace and judge and door. Yet, for all these names—which are to help us grasp the nature and range of His power—there is but one and the same Son of God who is our God.

These, then, are His names; but what are the meanings of these names? He is called the Word, first, to imply that He was begotten of the Father with no more passivity or substantial diminution in the Father than there is in a person who utters a spoken word; second, for the obvious reason that God the Father has always spoken through Him both to men and angels.

The name Wisdom tells us that in the beginning all things, through Him, were ordered wisely. He is the Light because it was He who brought light into the primordial darkness of the world and

Excerpts from entire essay.

145

who, by His coming among men, dissipated the darkness of their minds. Power is one of His names, since no created thing can ever overcome Him. He is right hand and arm, for through Him all things were made and by Him they are all sustained. He is called the angel of great counsel because He is the announcer of His Father's will.

He is said to be the Son of man because on our account He deigned to be born a man. He is called a lamb because of His perfect innocence; a sheep to symbolize His passion. For two reasons He is called a Priest: first, because He offered up His body as an oblation and victim to God the Father for us; second, because, through us, He condescends day after day to be offered up.

He is the Way along which we journey to our salvation; the Truth because He rejects what is false; the Life because He destroys death. He is a vine because He spreads out the branches of His arms that the world might pluck in clusters the grapes of consolation from the Cross. He is called Justice because through faith in His name sinners are made just; and Redemption because He paid the price in His blood to buy us back—we who had been so long lost. He is called bread because by His Gospel He fed the hunger of our ignorance; and a stone both because on Him the Serpent left no trace and because He afforded us protection.

146

He is the doctor who came to visit us and cured our weakness and our wounds; the fount of living water because by the "bath of regeneration" He cleanses sinners and gives them life. He is peace because He brought together those who lived apart, and reconciled us to God the Father. He is the Resurrection because He will raise all bodies from their graves; and the Judge because it is He who will judge both the living and the dead. He is the door because it is through Him that those who believe enter the kingdom of heaven.

These many names and titles belong to one Lord. Take courage, therefore, O man of faith, and plant your hope firmly in Him. If you would learn of the Father, listen to the Word. If you are saddened by persecution, take courage. Remember that He Himself went like a lamb to the slaughter. If you would be wise, ask Him who is Wisdom. If you find it hard to contemplate the High majesty of the Only-begotten, do not lose hope. Remember, He was made man to make it easy for men to approach Him.

Priest that He is, He will offer you as a victim to His Father. If you do not know the way of salvation, look for Christ, for He is the road of souls. If it is truth that you want, listen to Him, for He is the Truth. Have no fear whatever of death, for Christ is the Life of those who believe. Do the pleasures of the world entice you? Turn all the more to the Cross of Christ to find solace in the sweetness of the vine that clustered there.

If you are stumbling, fix your foot firmly on Him, for He is the rock. When you suffer from the ardors of passion, hurry to the well of life to put out the flame and to gain for your soul eternal life. Should anger torment you, and you be torn by the dissension of life, appeal to Christ who is peace, and you will be reconciled to the Father and will love everyone as you would like to be loved yourself. If you are afraid that your body is failing and have a dread of death, remember that He is the Resurrection and will raise up what has fallen.

PRUDENTIUS:

Hymns

Christ I sing whom king and prophet, crowned
    with priestly diadem
Long ago foretold with voice joined to sound
    of harp and drum,
Drinking of the Spirit from Heaven flowing
    deep into His soul.

Tell we now of deeds attested, marvels wrought
    by hand divine;
All the world is faithful witness, earth denies
    not what it saw
God in person come from Heaven, teaching
    men His holy way.

Of the Father's love begotten, long before the
    world began
Alpha and Omega titled, fount and term
    of all that is,
All that has before existed, all that shall
    hereafter be.

He assumed our fragile body, tainted members
    doomed to die
That the race from Adam springing might
    not perish in the end

Excerpts from *A Hymn for Every Hour*

149

Though a dreadful sentence plunged it
    deep in Hell's profound abyss.

O how blest that Birth supernal, when the
    Virgin Mother bore
Him who is the world's salvation, by the Holy
    Spirit conceived,
And the Infant, our Redeemer, showed to us
    His face divine.

Water poured into the tankards turns
    to rich Falernian wine,
And the waiter claims the vintage from the
    water-pots was drawn,
While the master with amazement tastes
    the cups of rosy hue.

Lazarus for four days buried, hidden in
    the sunless tomb,
He restores to life and vigor, giving
    power to breathe again,
And the soul returning, enters flesh
    now crumbling to decay.

Lo, He walks upon the waters, treads the
    crests of surging waves
And the deep in ceaseless motion makes
    a pathway insecure
But the billows dare not open under-
    neath His sacred feet.

150

Lift my soul, your tuneful voice, let
    the tongue be swift to praise,
Tell the victory of the Passion, tell the triumph
    of the Cross,
Sing the Sign that gleams refulgent, marked
    upon the Christian's brow.

For awhile salvation's Leader gave Himself
    to realms of death,
That He might the dead, long buried, guide
    in their return to light,
When the chains that had been welded by that
    primal sin were loosed.

Then, in steps of their Creator, many saints
    and patriarchs,
Putting on their fleshy garments and arising
    from their tombs,
Followed Him, at length returning on the
    third day to the earth.

Chapter 5

THE

KINGDOM

OF

GOD

To them also He showed
Himself alive after His passion
by many proofs, during forty
days appearing to them and
speaking to them of the Kingdom
of God.

Acts 1:3

Our Lord's kingdom was not of this world, yet it must be in this world. It was a spiritual kingdom that must be very active in the world of each generation, a dynamic society that would lead all men to God. This was the vision of the late Pope John XXIII when he called for a New Pentecost, a new outpouring of the Holy Spirit to redeem our times. This is the vision of a Father Alberione who has founded religious and secular institutes to meet the twentieth century world and win it for Christ.

For the Kingdom of God embraces men and women living in the world and raises them up to heaven. It is a spiritual world, a foretaste of heaven itself, feeding men the spiritual nourishment of divine truths and God-given Sacraments. This kingdom gives men a share of the Christ-life, starting with the rebirth of Baptism. It teaches men to pray, to repent, to forgive. It teaches them to see beyond the veil of time into eternity, to love their fellowmen even at great sacrifice, to share in all charity.

The Kingdom of God, in this world, is solidly founded on the rock upon which Christ formed it—St. Peter and his successors. It is anchored in Christ for all eternity, since He is the head of the Mystical Body. In the deposit of faith which it treasures, preserves, and pours out, it remembers all the things Christ taught during those forty days after His resurrection when He appeared to the apostles and spoke to them of His Kingdom. Christ is truly a King, and He invites us to reign with Him.

ST. AMBROSE:

The Mysteries

I see waters which I used to see daily. Are these able to cleanse me, into which I have often descended and have never been cleansed? From this, learn that water cleanses not without the Spirit.

And so you have read that the three witnesses in baptism are one: the water, the blood and the Spirit, for, if you take away one of these, the sacrament of baptism does not stand. For what is water without the cross of Christ except a common element without any sacramental effect? And again, without water there is no mystery of regeneration, for, "Unless a man be born again of water and the Spirit, he cannot enter into the kingdom of God." Moreover, even a catechumen believes in the cross of the Lord Jesus, with which he, too, is signed, but, unless he be baptized "in the name of the Father and of the Son and of the Holy Spirit," he cannot receive remission of sins nor drink in the benefit of spiritual grace.

Therefore, that Syrian (Naaman) dipped seven times under the law, but you were baptized in the name of the Trinity; you confessed the Father, you confessed the Son, you confessed the Spirit. Retain

Excerpts from chapters 19-24; 45-46

the order of things. In this faith you died to the world, you arose to God, and, as if buried in that element of the world, dead to sin you were revived to eternal life. Believe, therefore, that these waters are not without power.

Therefore, it is said to you: "An angel of the Lord used to come down at certain times into the pool and the water was moved, and the first to go down into the pool after the troubling of the water was healed of whatever infirmity he had." This pool was in Jerusalem, in which one was healed every year. But no one was healed before the angel had descended. So the angel descended and, that there might be a sign that the angel had come down, the water was moved. The water was moved because of the unbelievers; for them a sign, for you faith; for them an angel came down, for you the Holy Spirit; for them a creature was moved, for you Christ operates, the Lord of the creature. Then one was cured; now all are healed.

Finally, the paralytic was awaiting a man. Who was He but the Lord Jesus born of the Virgin, at whose coming no longer would the shadow heal men one by one, but the truth who would heal all men together. This then, was the one whose descent was being waited for, of whom God the Father said to John the Baptist, "Upon whom thou wilt see the Spirit descending from heaven and abiding upon Him, He it is who baptizes with the Holy Spirit," of whom John has testified, saying: "I saw the Holy Spirit descending from heaven as a dove and remaining upon Him." Why did the Spirit here descend like a dove, except that you might see, except that you might know, that you might recognize the type of the mystery. The dove, also, which the just Noe sent forth from the ark was the likeness of this dove.

The lesson from Genesis which has been read teaches also in types. After Abraham had conquered his enemies and had received back his own nephew, when he was enjoying victory, then Melchisedech met him and brought forth those things which Abraham venerated and received. Abraham did not bring them forth, but Melchisedech, who is introduced "without father, without mother, having neither beginning of days nor end, but like to the Son of God," of whom Paul says to the Hebrews: "He continues a priest forever," who in the Latin version is called King of Justice, King of Peace.

Do you not recognize who this is? Can a man be a king of justice, when he himself is scarcely just; can he be a king of peace, when he can scarcely be peaceable? "Without a mother" according to divinity, because He was begotten of God the Father, of one substance with the Father; "without a father" according to the Incarnation, because He was born of the Virgin, "having neither a beginning nor end," for He himself is "the beginning and the end" of all things, "the first and the last." Therefore, the sacrament which you have received is not a gift of man but of God, brought forth by Him who blessed Abraham, the father of the faith, him whose grace and deeds you admire.

ST. BASIL:

Homily on Psalm 28

"The Lord is upon many waters." Ps. 28:3.

We have learned in the creation of the world that there is water above the heavens, again, water of the deep, and yet again, the gathered waters of the seas. Who, then, is He who controls these waters except the Lord who established Himself upon all things, who holds sway over the waters?

Perhaps, even in a more mystic manner, the voice of the Lord was upon the waters, when a voice from above came to Jesus as He was baptized, "This is my beloved Son." At that time, truly the Lord was upon many waters, making the waters holy through baptism; but, the God of majesty thundered from above with a mighty voice of testimony. And over those to be baptized a voice left behind by the Lord is pronounced: "Go, therefore," it says, "baptize in the name of the Father, and of the Son, and of the Holy Spirit." Therefore, "The voice of the Lord is upon the waters."

"And he shall reduce them to pieces as a calf of Libanus." Ps. 28:6.

Excerpts from sections 3 and 5

Remember the calf in Exodus, which they fashioned through idolatry, which Moses beat to powder and gave the people to drink. In a manner similar to that of the calf, Christ will utterly destroy the practice of idolatry.

"And as the beloved son of unicorns." Ps. 28:6.

The Only-begotten Son, He who gives His life for the world whenever He offers Himself as a sacrifice and oblation to God for sins, is called both Lamb of God and a Sheep. "Behold," it is said, "the lamb of God." And again: "He was led like a sheep to slaughter." But when it was necessary to take vengeance and to overthrow the power attacking the race of men, a certain wild and savage force, then He will be called the Son of unicorns.

For, as we have learned in Job, the unicorn is is a creature, irresistible in might and unsubjected to man. "For, thou canst not bind him with a thong," he says, "nor will he stay at thy crib." There is also much said in that part of the prophecy about the animal acting like a free man and not submitting to men. It has been observed that the Scripture has used the comparison of the unicorn in both ways, at one time in praise, at another in censure.

"Deliver," he says, "my soul from the sword . . . and my lowness from the horns of the unicorns." He said these words complaining of the warlike people who in the time of passion rose up in rebellion against him. Again he says, "My horn shall be exalted like that of the unicorn." It seems that on account of the promptness of the animal in repelling attacks, it is frequently found representing the baser things, and because of its high horn and freedom, it is assigned to represent the better. On the whole, since it is possible to find the "horn" used in Scripture in many places instead of "glory" and "power," Christ is called the Unicorn on the ground that He has common power and glory with the Father.

Concerning Baptism

But perhaps we should now proceed to another consideration and, by our faith in Christ, to arrive at the knowledge and understanding of what it means to be baptized in the Name of the Father and of the Son and of the Holy Spirit. First of all, it is necessary to point out that the special glory of the Person named is signified by each name. Secondly, it must be borne in mind that the Lord Himself revealed the significance of Baptism in the name of the Holy Spirit when He said, "That which is born of the flesh is flesh, and that which is born of the spirit is spirit."

Thus, with the familiar instance of the continuity of reproduction which obtains in carnal birth as an illustration, we may acquire a clear and accurate understanding of religious doctrine. We know, indeed, and are fully convinced that just as that which is born of flesh shares the nature of that of which it has been born, so also, we who are born of the Spirit are, necessarily, spirit. But this spirit is not according to the great glory of the Holy Spirit which cannot be comprehended by the human

Excerpts from Book 1, chapter 2

mind, but it is according to the glory which is in the distribution to every man for his profit of the gifts of God, through His Christ.

It is mysteriously discerned also in the operation of all these gifts and in other instances, by words, likewise; as when we recall to memory the commandments of God which were proclaimed through our Lord Jesus Christ, who also said, "He himself will teach you all things and bring all things to your mind, whatsoever I shall have said to you." Then, too, the Apostle tells us at greater length what the attitudes of mind are whereby a man becomes spirit. In one place he writes, "But the fruit of the spirit is charity, joy, peace, patience," and so on. Previously he had said, "But if you are led by the Spirit you are not under the Law," and in another place, "If we live by the Spirit, let us also walk in the Spirit."

In these and other passages of the kind, then, the Lord says that they who are born of the Spirit become spirit. The Apostle again testifies to the same truth when he says, "For this cause I bow my knees to the Father of our Lord Jesus Christ, of whom all paternity in heaven and earth is named, that he would grant you, according to the riches of his glory, to be strengthened by His Spirit with might unto the inward man."

And if, living in the Spirit, we also walk in the Spirit, thus becoming receptive of the Holy Spirit, we shall be enabled to confess Christ—because "No man can say 'Jesus is Lord' except by the Holy Spirit." In this way, therefore, the Lord, both by His own words and through His apostle taught that they who are born of the Spirit become spirit.

And in this spiritual regeneration we shall again imitate birth according to the flesh, in that first, we change our abode and alter our ways by strengthening the inner man in spirit, so that we can say now, "But our conversation is in heaven." While we draw our body along upon the earth, we keep our souls in the company of heavenly spirits. Secondly, we change our companions, for David says, "The man that in private detracted his neighbor, him did I persecute. With him that had a proud eye and an insatiable heart, I would not eat. My eyes were upon the faithful of the earth, to sit with me," and similarly in other places.

And the Apostle tells us clearly of the new manner of life to which we are called, prefacing his words by speaking of the great and glorious grace of Christ's mercy. He says, "For he is our peace, who hath made both one, and breaking down the middle wall of partition, the enmities in his flesh; making void the law of commandments contained in the decrees; that he might make the two in himself into one new man, making peace; and might reconcile both to God in one body by the cross; killing the enmities in himself. And coming, he preached peace to you that were afar off, and peace to them that were nigh. For by Him we have access both in one Spirit to the Father. Now, therefore, you are no longer strangers and foreigners, but you are fellow citizens with the saints and the domestics of God, built upon the foundation of the Apostles and prophets, Jesus Christ Himself being the chief cornerstone; in whom all the building being framed together, groweth up into a holy temple in the Lord."

And so, planted together with Christ in the likeness of His death, baptized in the name of the Holy Spirit, born anew as to the inner man in newness of mind, and built upon the foundation of the Apostles and prophets, we may be made worthy to be baptized in the name of the Only-begotten Son of God and merit to receive the great grace of which the Apostle speaks when he says, "As many of you as have been baptized in Christ have put on Christ." "There is neither Gentile nor Jew, circumcision nor uncircumcision, barbarian nor Scythian, bond nor free. But Christ is all and in all."

Now, it follows necessarily that he who has been born must also be clothed. Consider, for example, a drawing tablet. It may be fashioned of any sort of material; it may be irregularly cut or the surface left unplaned. If it bears a drawing of the king, the difference in material—whether it be wood or gold or silver—does not affect the drawing. The accurate resemblance of the image to its model and its artistic and meticulous presentation make the difference in material pass unnoticed, however obvious this difference may be. The spectators are moved to admire the excellence of the likeness.

The case is the same with one who is baptized, whether he be Jew or Gentile, male or female, slave or free, Scythian or barbarian, or anyone else bearing the name of any other race. As soon as he has put off the old man with his deeds in the blood of Christ and, by Christ's teaching, has put on the new man, created according to God in justice and holiness of truth, and is renewed unto knowledge according to the very image of the Creator, he becomes worthy to win the divine approval, of which the Apostle speaks when he says, "And we know that to them who love God, all things work together unto good, to such as, according to his purpose, are called. For, whom he foreknew, he also predestined to be made conformable to the image of His Son; that he might be the firstborn amongst many brethren."

Then, when the soul has been born again of the Spirit, and clothed with the Son of God, it becomes worthy of the final and perfect stage and is baptized in the name of the Father Himself of our Lord Jesus Christ, who, according to John, gave us the power to be made sons of God. This power is granted by the grace of our Lord Jesus Christ Himself, the Only-begotten Son of the living God, in whom "neither circumcision availeth anything nor uncircumcision, but faith that worketh by charity," as it is written.

Through this grace we successfully accomplish that command which is added to the precept of baptism by the same Jesus Christ, our Lord. He says, "Teaching them to observe all things, whatsoever I have commanded you." Moreover, the Lord Himself declared that the observance of His commands is the proof of our love for Him, saying, "If you love me, keep my commandments." And again, "He that hath my commandments and keepeth them, he it is that loveth me;" and yet again, "If anyone love me, he will keep my word and my Father will love him."

And with still greater force and importunity, He says, "Abide in my love. If you keep my commandments, you shall abide in my love; as I also have kept my Father's commandments and do abide in His love." Now, if the observance of the commandments is the essential sign of love, it is greatly to be feared that without love, even the most effective action of the glorious gifts of grace will be of no avail. Thus Paul himself declares, "If I speak with the tongues of men and angels, and have not charity, I am become as sounding brass or a tinkling cymbal. And if I should have prophecy and should know all mysteries and all knowledge, and if I should have all faith, so that I could remove mountains, and have not charity, I am nothing."

TERTULLIAN:

On Prayer

Our Lord knew that He alone was without sin. Therefore, He taught us to say in prayer: "Forgive us our trespasses." A prayer for pardon is an acknowledgment of sin, since one who asks pardon confesses his guilt. Thus, too, repentance is shown to be acceptable to God, because God wills this rather than the death of the sinner.

Now, in Scripture, "debt" is used figuratively to mean sin, because of this analogy: When a man owes something to a judge and payment is exacted from him, he does not escape the just demand unless excused from the payment of the debt, just as the master forgave the debt to the servant. Now, this is the point of the whole parable: Just as the servant was freed by his lord, but failed in turn to be merciful to his debtor and therefore, when brought before his lord, was handed over to the torturer until he paid the last penny, that is, the least and last of his faults, Christ intended by this parable to get us, also, to forgive our debtors.

This is expressed elsewhere under this aspect of prayer; "Forgive," He said, "and you shall be forgiven." And when Peter asked if one should forgive

Excerpts from chapter 7, ff.

his brother seven times, our Lord said, "Rather, seventy times seven times," that He might improve upon the Law, for in Genesis vengeance was demanded of Cain seven times, of Lamech seventy times seven.

To complete the prayer which was so well arranged, Christ added that we should pray not only that our sins be forgiven, but that they be shunned completely: "Lead us not into temptation," that is, do not allow us to be led by the Tempter. Christ Himself was tempted by the devil and pointed out the subtle director of the temptation. This passage He confirms later when He says: "Pray that you may not enter into temptation." They were so tempted to desert their Lord because they had indulged in sleep instead of prayer. Therefore, the phrase which balances and interprets "Lead us not into temptation" is "But deliver us from evil."

How many utterances of the Prophets, Evangelists, and Apostles; how many of our Lord's sermons, parables, examples and precepts are touched in the brief compass of a few little words! How many duties are fulfilled. The honor due to God in the word "Father"; a testimony of faith in the very title used; the offering of obedience in the mention of God's will; the remembrance of hope in the mention of His kingdom; a petition for life in the mention of bread; the confession of sins in asking for pardon; solicitude regarding temptation in the request for protection.

Yet, why be surprised? God alone could teach us how He would have us pray. The homage of prayer, then, as arranged by Him and animated by His Spirit at the very moment it went forth from His divine lips, because of the prerogative granted to Him, ascends to heaven, recommending to the Father what the Son has taught.

Since, however, our Lord, who saw the needs of men, after giving them the method of prayer, said, "Ask and you shall receive," and since every man has petitions to make according to his own circumstances, everyone first sends ahead the prescribed and customary prayer which will, so to speak, lay the groundwork for his additional desires. Then he may add petitions, over and above—ever keeping in mind, however, the prescribed conditions, that we may be no farther from the ears of God than from His teachings.

For what will God refuse to the prayer that comes to Him from the spirit and in truth, since this is the prayer He has exacted. What proofs of its efficacy do we read of and hear of and believe! Prayer alone overcomes God; but Christ has conferred upon it all power for good. Prayer has the power to make the weak recover, to heal the sick, to open prison doors, to loosen the chains of the innocent. It likewise remits sins, repels temptations, stamps out persecution, consoles, delights, calms, sustains and supports us.

Prayer is the wall of faith, our shield and weapons against the foe who studies us from all sides. Hence, let us never set forth unarmed. Let us be mindful of our guard-duty by day and our vigil by night. Beneath the arms of prayer let us guard the standard of our general, and let us pray as we await the bugle call of the angel.

What need, then, is there of further discussion of the duty of prayer? Even our Lord Himself prayed, to whom be honor and power forever and ever.

ST. CAESARIUS OF ARLES:

On the Lord's Prayer

As often as we celebrate any sacred feasts, dearly beloved, and prepare to receive Holy Communion, you know with what dispositions we should come. Before we come, you are well aware of what we should first say to God in prayer: "Forgive us our debts, as we also forgive our debtors." See to it that you grant forgiveness, for you will come to those words in the prayer.

How are you going to say them? Or will you, perhaps, not do so? Finally I ask: Are you saying them or not? You hate your brother and say: "Forgive us as we also forgive." You will answer: I do not say them. You pray, and do not say them? Listen, and pay close attention. Soon you are to pray; grant forgiveness from your heart. Do you quarrel with your enemy? First quarrel with your own heart.

Say to your heart: Do not hate. How shall I pray? How shall I say: "Forgive us our debts"? This we can say indeed, but how are we to say what follows: "as we also forgive." You are unwilling to

Excerpts from Sermon 35

forgive, and your soul is sad because you are telling it to hate nothing. Say to it, in turn: "Why art thou sad?" Do not ruin me by hatred.

You grow faint, you pant, you are wounded with grief, you cannot remove the hatred from your heart. "Hope in God." He is the Physician. He hung on the cross for you and still is not an avenger. Why do you want to take vengeance? For that is why you bear hatred, in order to get revenge. Look at Him hanging on the cross and with His Blood effecting a cure for you in your weakness. Do you want revenge? Look at Christ hanging there and listen to Him pray: "Father, forgive them, for they do not know what they are doing."

However, you say to me: He could do it, but I cannot; I am a man, He is God. If you cannot imitate Christ, why did the blessed Apostle Peter say: "Christ also has suffered for you, leaving you an example that you may follow in His steps." And why did the Apostle Paul exclaim: "Be you imitators of God, as very dear children"? Moreover, why did Our Lord Himself say: "Learn from Me, for I am meek and humble of heart"?

To plead in our own defense we say that we cannot do what we are completely unwilling to do. It is true that we cannot imitate Christ in all things. You cannot imitate Him in raising the dead to life and performing other acts, but you can imitate Christ in meekness and humility of heart. Be kind and merciful; possess true charity; love not only your friends, but your enemies. If you do this, you will follow in the footsteps of your Lord.

Do you still say that you cannot fulfill any of these things I mentioned—being kind and merciful, observing chastity, and loving all men as oneself? Indeed, if we only set our minds to it, we can do all of them with God's help. When a man comes before the tribunal of Christ, it will be utterly impossible to make excuses, for no one could know our capabilities better than He who gave them to us. Moreover, God who is just could not command the impossible, and in His goodness He will not condemn a man for what was unavoidable.

Now, if we say that we cannot fulfill Christ's commands, we assert that He gave orders that were too harsh and impossible of fulfillment. It would be better to say in all humility with the Prophet: "Thou art just, O God: and thy judgment is just." Thou art good, we are wicked; Thou, merciful, we, hard-hearted. When we say this let us pray with our whole heart that He may give us the ability to carry out His commands.

Now, all these things which I mentioned before—to scorn the desires of this world, to observe perfect charity toward all men, to love not only friends but also enemies—can be accomplished with God's help, provided we try to uproot from our hearts unlawful desires, the mother of all vices. Indeed, the greater the abundance of things, the more the need of them increases.

Truly, the fault does not lie with silver and gold. Let a kind man find a treasure and through the prompting of his kindness, hospitality is offered to strangers, the hungry are fed, the naked clothed, the poor helped and spiritual riches are stored up in heaven. Who does this sort of thing? The good, kind man. With what? Silver and gold. Whom does he serve? The One who said: "The gold is mine, and the silver is mine." Know well, dearly beloved, that riches cannot harm a good man because he uses them kindly; likewise, they cannot help the wicked man as long as he keeps them avariciously or wastes them in dissipation.

Therefore, let us learn to love God with our whole heart, and let us begin to love all men as ourselves. If we do this, no strife over earthly possessions, no scandal, no quarrels will ever be able to separate us from the love of God and of our neighbor. Indeed, how will it be possible for anyone to do wrong if he loves all men as himself with perfect charity? Love all men with your whole heart, and do whatever you wish. Love those who are just because they are good, and pray that they will become better. Love also those who are wicked because they are men, and hate the fact that they are evil.

Moreover, always desire that God in His goodness may convert them to good works. Then, if you long to possess the riches of perfect charity, you will consider the pleasures of earthly desires as nothing. Truly, what does the rich man have if he does not possess charity. Therefore, let us seek after the riches of charity with all our might. Then we will happily arrive at eternal bliss where there are true riches, with the help of our Lord Jesus Christ, to whom is honor and power.

ST. CYPRIAN:

The Unity of the Church

Proof for faith is easy in a brief statement of the truth. The Lord speaks to Peter: "I say to thee," He says, "thou art Peter, and upon this rock I will build my church, and the gates of hell shall not prevail against it. And I will give thee the keys of the kingdom of heaven; and whatever thou shalt bind on earth shall be bound also in heaven, and whatever thou shalt loose on earth shall be loosed also in heaven." Upon him, being one, He builds His Church, and although after His Resurrection He bestows equal power upon all the Apostles, and says: "As the Father has sent me, I also send you. Receive ye the Holy Spirit: if you forgive the sins of anyone, they will be forgiven him; if you retain the sins of anyone, they will be retained," yet that He might display unity, He established by His authority the origin of the same unity as beginning from one.

Surely the rest of the Apostles also were that which Peter was, endowed with an equal partnership of office and of power, but the beginning proceeds from unity, that the Church of Christ may be shown to be one. This one Church, also, the

Excerpts from chapters 4, 6, 7.

Holy Spirit in the Canticle of Canticles designates in the Person of the Lord and says: "One is my dove, my perfect one is but one, she is the only one of her mother, the chosen of her that bore her." Does he who does not hold this unity think that he holds the faith? Does he who strives against the Church and resists her think that he is in the Church? The blessed apostle Paul teaches this same thing and sets forth the sacrament of unity saying: "One body and one Spirit, one hope of your calling, one Lord, one faith, one baptism, one God."

The spouse of Christ cannot be defiled; she is uncorrupted and chaste. She knows one home, with chaste modesty she guards the sanctity of one couch. She keeps us for God; she assigns the children whom she has created to the kingdom. Whoever is separated from the Church and is joined with an adulteress is separated from the promises of the Church, nor will he who has abandoned the Church arrive at the rewards of Christ. He is a stranger; he is profane; he is an enemy.

He cannot have God as a father who does not have the Church as a mother. The Lord says, "He who is not with me is against me, and who does not gather with me, scatters. He who breaks the peace and concord of Christ acts against Christ; he who gathers somewhere outside the Church scatters the Church of Christ.

The Lord said: "I and the Father are one." And again of the Father and Son and Holy Spirit it is written: "And these three are one." Does anyone believe that this unity which comes from divine strength, which is closely connected with the divine sacraments, can be broken asunder in the Church and be separated by the divisions of colliding wills? He who does not hold this unity, does not hold the law of God, does not hold the faith of the Father and the Son, does not hold life and salvation.

This sacrament of unity, this bond of concord inseparably connected is shown, when in the Gospel the tunic of the Lord Jesus Christ is not at all divided and is not torn, but by those who cast lots for the garment of Christ a sound garment is received. He cannot possess the garment of Christ who tears and divides the Church of Christ. Even under the symbol of His garment, Christ shows the unity of His Church.

ST. JOHN CHRYSOSTOM:

Homilies on John

St. Peter says, "To whom shall we go? Thou hast the words of everlasting life, and we have come to believe and to know that thou art the Christ, the Son of the living God." These words were indicative of a great and tender love, for they showed that the Master was dearer to them than all else—father and mother and all the rest—and that, if they departed from Him, they had nowhere to go for refuge.

And St. Peter at once added, "Thou hast words of everlasting life." Some, to be sure, listened to Christ carnally, and with human reasonings, but the Apostles heard Him spiritually and entrusted all His teachings to faith. That is why Christ said: "The words that I have spoken to you are spirit;" that is, "Do not conceive the notion that My doctrine is subject to the sequence of events and the necessity of human things. Spiritual things are not of this kind and are not constrained to be enslaved by the laws of earth."

"Thou hast the words of eternal life." They had already accepted the resurrection and all that will

Excerpts from the 47th homily.

180

be appointed therein. And see how this lover of the brethren, this warm hearted friend, spoke out in the name of the whole group, for he did not say, "I know," but "We know." And more than this, notice how he came near using the very words of the Master, not of the adversaries. They had said, "This is the son of Joseph," while Peter said: "Thou art the Christ, the Son of the living God," and "Thou hast words of everlasting life," perhaps because he had often heard Him saying: "He who believes in Me has everlasting life." Indeed, by recalling His very words he showed that he cherished all that Christ said.

What did Christ do then? He did not praise Peter; He did not show special admiration, though He did this on other occasions. On the contrary, what did He say this time? "Have I not chosen you, the Twelve? Yet one of you is a devil." Because Peter had said: "We have come to believe," Christ excluded Judas from the group.

Why, then, did He say: "Have I not chosen you, the Twelve? Yet one of you is a devil"? To show that His teaching was not in any way colored by flattery. Since they alone remained after all had left Him, and they were acknowledging through Peter that He was the Christ, in order that they might not think that on this account He was going to cater to them, He did away with the possibility of their entertaining this notion.

What He meant is something like this: "Nothing keeps Me from reproving the wicked; do not think that because you have remained with Me I shall not find fault with you if you do wrong." God is not wont to make men good by compulsion and force, and His election and choice are not coercive of those called, but rather, persuasive. And that you may learn that the vocation does not coerce, consider how many of those called have been lost. It is plain from this that salvation and damnation lie in our will.

Therefore, when we hear these things, let us learn always to be careful and vigilant. If Judas who was classed among that saintly company, who had enjoyed so great a gift, who had worked miracles, when he had become infected with the dread evil of greed, even betrayed his own Master, and neither his good works nor his gifts helped him—let us fear that we may imitate Judas by avarice.

You do not betray Christ? When you neglect a poor man wasted with hunger, or perishing with cold, you are liable to the same punishment as Judas. And when we partake of the Mysteries unworthily, we are lost in the same way as those who kill

Christ. When we rob, when we despoil those weaker than we, we shall draw upon ourselves the greatest punishment.

"But," you object, "is it not a good thing to build fine houses and look up at a golden roof?" In all truth, it is a vain and foolish thing. Do you wish to see a most beautiful ceiling? As evening descends, look at the sky adorned with stars. "But that is not my ceiling," you will say. But it is yours much more than that other.

And I say this because it has been made for you and is yours in common with your brothers, while the other is not yours, but belongs to your heirs after your death. Besides, the one can be of the greatest assistance by drawing you to the Creator by its beauty, while the other will be of the greatest harm to you by becoming your most powerful accuser on the day of judgment since it itself has been covered with gold, while Christ in His brothers has not had even the necessary clothing.

ST. BASIL:

Homily on Psalm 44

"Thou art ripe in beauty, above the sons of men." Ps. 44:3.

Now David calls the Lord ripe in beauty above the sons of men when he fixes his gaze on His divinity. He does not celebrate the beauty of the flesh. "And we have seen Him, and He had no sightliness, nor beauty, but His appearance was without honor and lacking above the sons of men." It is evident, then, that the prophet, looking upon His brilliancy and being filled with the splendor there, his soul smitten with this beauty, was moved to a divine love of the spiritual beauty, and when this appeared to the human soul all things hitherto loved seemed shameful and abominable.

Therefore, even St. Paul, when he saw His ripe beauty "counted all things as dung that he might gain Christ." Those outside the word of truth, despising the simplicity of expression in the Scriptures, call the preaching of the Gospel folly; but we, who glory in the cross of Christ, "to whom the gifts bestowed on us by God were manifested

Excerpts from sections 4, 5.

through the Spirit, not in words taught by human wisdom," know that the grace poured out by God in the teachings concerning Christ is rich.

Therefore, in a short time the teaching passed through almost the whole world, since grace, rich and plentiful, was poured out upon the preachers of the Gospel, whom Scripture called the lips of Christ. Moreover, the message of the Gospel in its insignificant little words possesses great guidance and attraction toward salvation. And every soul is overcome by the unalterable doctrines, being strengthened by grace to an unshaken faith in Christ. Whence the Apostle says: "Through whom we have received grace and apostleship to bring about obedience to faith." And again: "I have labored more than any of them, yet not I, but the grace of God with me."

"Grace is poured abroad in Thy lips; therefore hath God blessed Thee forever." Ps. 44:3 (cont.).

In the Gospel it has been written: "They marvelled at the words of grace that came from His mouth." The psalm, wishing to bring forward vividly the great amount of grace in the words spoken by Our Lord says: "Grace is poured abroad in Thy lips," because of the abundance of grace in His words.

"God hath blessed Thee forever," it says. It is evident that these words refer to His human nature, as it advances "in wisdom and age and grace." According to this we clearly perceive that grace has been given to Him as the prize for His brave deeds. "Thou hast loved justice and hated iniquity: therefore God, thy God, hath anointed Thee with the oil of gladness above Thy fellows." Ps. 44:8.

The saying of Paul to the Philippians is also much like this: "He humbled Himself, becoming obedient to death, even to death on a cross. Therefore God also has exalted Him." It is clear that these words are spoken concerning the Savior as a man.

Or there is this explanation. Since the Church is the Body of the Lord, and He Himself is the head of the Church, so also we, as many of us as are believers, are the other members of the Body of Christ. Now, if anyone refers to the Lord the praise given to the Church, he will not sin. Therefore the sayings "God hath blessed Thee," and "anointed Thee above Thy fellows," apply to the Church.

"Gird Thy sword upon Thy thigh, O Thou most mighty. With Thy ripeness and Thy beauty." Ps. 44:4

We believe that this refers figuratively to the living Word of God, so that He is joined with the flesh, who is "efficient and keener than any two-edged sword, and extending even to the division of soul and spirit, of joints also and of marrow, and a discerner of the thoughts and intentions of the heart." For the thigh is a symbol of efficiency in generation. "For these," he says, "are the souls that came out of Jacob's thigh."

As, then, Our Lord Jesus Christ is a life and a way, and bread and a grapevine and a true light, and is also called numberless other names, so, too, He is a sword that cuts through the sensual part of the soul and mortifies the motions of concupiscence.

Then, since God the Word was about to unite Himself to the weakness of the flesh, there is added beautifully the expression "Thou most mighty," because the fact that God was able to exist in the nature of man bears proof of the greatest power. In fact, the construction of heaven and earth, and the generation of sea and air and the greatest elements, and whatever is known above the earth and whatever beneath the earth, do not commend the power of the Word of God as much as His dispensation concerning the Incarnation and His condescension to the lowliness and weakness of humanity.

ST. CLEMENT OF ROME:

Letter to the Corinthians

For Christ belongs to the humble-minded, not to those who exalt themselves above His flock. The scepter of the majesty of God, the Lord Jesus Christ, came not in the pomp of boasting or of arrogance, though He was mighty; but He was humble-minded as the Holy Spirit spoke concerning Him.

For He says, "Lord, who has believed our report, and to whom is the arm of the Lord revealed? We announced in His presence—He is as a Child, as a root in thirsty ground. There is no beauty in Him, nor comeliness, and we have seen Him and He had neither form nor beauty." You see, beloved, what is the example given to us. For if the Lord was thus humble-minded, what shall we do who through Him have come under the yoke of His grace?

This is the way, beloved, by which we found our Savior, Jesus Christ, the high priest of our offerings, the protector and helper of our weakness. Through Him, let us strain our eyes toward the heights of heaven; through Him we see mirrored

Excerpts from chapters 16, 36, 42, and 49, and the conclusion.

The Lord (particular) Fra Angelico
Museum of St. Mark, Florence

"The Lord Jesus Christ came not in the pomp of boasting
or of arrogance, though He was mighty; but He was
humble-minded as the Holy Spirit spoke concerning Him."

St. Clement of Rome

His spotless and glorious countenance. Through Him, the eyes of our heart have been opened; through Him our foolish and darkened understanding shoots up into the light; through Him the Lord willed that we should taste immortal knowledge, "Who, being the brightness of His majesty, is so much greater than the angels as He hath inherited a more excellent name."

For it is so written, "Who makes His angels spirits, and His ministers a flame of fire." But regarding His Son the Lord has spoken thus: "Thou art My Son, this day have I begotten Thee. Ask of Me, I will give Thee the gentiles for Thy inheritance, and the end of the earth for Thy possession." And again He says to Him: "Sit on My right hand until I make Thy enemies a footstool for Thy feet." Who then are the enemies? They who are wicked and resist His will.

The Apostles received the Gospel for us from the Lord Jesus Christ; Jesus Christ was sent from God. Christ, therefore, is from God and the Apostles are from Christ. Both, accordingly, came in proper order by the will of God. Receiving their orders, therefore, and being filled with confidence because of the Resurrection of the Lord Jesus Christ, and confirmed in the Word of God, with full assurance of the Holy Spirit, they went forth preaching the Gospel of the Kingdom of God that was about to come. Preaching, accordingly, throughout the country and the cities, they appointed their first-fruits, after testing them by the Spirit, to be bishops and deacons of those who should believe.

In charity, then, the Lord received us; out of the charity which He had for us, Jesus Christ Our Lord gave His blood for us by the will of God, and His flesh for our flesh, and His life for our lives.

Who can explain the bond of the charity of God? Who can express the splendor of its beauty? The height to which charity lifts us is inexpressible. Charity unites us to God, "Charity covers a multitude of sins"; charity bears all things, is long-suffering in all things. There is nothing mean in charity, nothing arrogant. Charity knows no schism, does not rebel, does all things in concord. In charity, all the elect of God have been made perfect. Without charity, nothing is pleasing to God.

May the all-seeing God and ruler of the spirits and Lord of all flesh, who chose the Lord Jesus Christ and us through Him to be a special people, grant to every soul upon whom His great and holy name has been invoked, faith, fear, peace, patience, and long-suffering, self-control, purity and prudence, so that they may be well-pleasing to His name through our high priest and defender Jesus Christ, through whom be glory and majesty, power and honor, to Him, both now and for all ages. Amen.

Chapter 6

MAN

OF

SORROWS

Despised, and the most
abject of men, a man of
sorrows, and acquainted
with infirmity: and His
look was as it were hidden
and despised, whereupon we
esteemed Him not.

Isaias 53:3

*The Gospels relate the stark details of Christ's passion and death.
The Evangelists write like men still in shock over witnessing the
crime of deicide. Isaias must give us, in the poignant beauty of
prophecy, a different insight into this most noble of sacrifices.*

193

For when Christ was lifted up on the cross, He drew all men to Himself. The erection of mankind to share in the sacrifice of Christ, the invitation to share His victimhood, meant a sharing in His reward, a pledge of future immortality in the Resurrection of Christ. The glory that He received from the Father He longs to share with us, since this unprecedented act of love was offered for us.

This sacrifice went infinitely beyond the bounds needed to redeem us. One prayer, one act of charity or humility or obedience would have been sufficient to save all mankind. Indeed, one drop of His precious Blood would have been a superabundant price, worthy of a superabundant reward. In His circumcision, alone, there was sufficient sacrifice to redeem all of rational creation.

Yet, this would not satisfy infinite Love. Christ must pour Himself out completely for us. He must become the Man of Sorrows, despised, and the most abject of men. He must bear our infirmities and carry our sorrows, be wounded and bruised for our sins, to prove forever the infinite heights of His love for us. Who, indeed, will believe our report! Is it any wonder that St. Paul wanted to preach Christ—Christ Crucified!

Can such love be vainly brought us? What must be our response?

ST. JOHN CHRYSOSTOM:

Homilies on St. John

"Then Pilate handed him over to them to be crucified. And so they took Jesus and led him away. And bearing the cross for himself, he went forth to the place called the Skull, in Hebrew Golgotha, where they crucified him."

Prosperity has a way of bringing about the downfall and complete dissolution of the unwary. Thus, the Jews, who from the beginning enjoyed the favor of God, repeatedly turned to the law of the Kingdom of the Gentiles, and when they were in the desert, after receiving manna, they kept recalling onions! In the same way, in this instance, also, they spurned the Kingdom of Christ and called on that of Caesar for support.

Accordingly, when Pilate heard the charges, he handed Christ to the Romans to be crucified—and was acting very illogically in this. For, though he ought to have investigated whether Christ had really tried to overthrow the government, motivated by fear alone, he tacitly consented to the charge, even though Christ, in anticipation of this, and to protect him from this blunder, had declared: "My kingdom is not of this world." However, surrender-

Excerpts from the 85th Homily.

ing himself completely to the interests of this world, though his wife's dream must have terrified him greatly, Pilate had no desire to do right to the point of heroism. On the contrary, nothing influenced him for the better and he handed Christ over to be crucified.

They placed the cross on Christ's shoulders as if on one accursed. Now, this was also the case in Type, for Isaac carried the wood for the sacrifice. At that time, however, the sacrifice took place only insofar as being willed by the father (for it was a type merely), while now it was taking place in actuality, for it was the fulfillment of the type.

"And he came to the place called the Skull." Some say that there Adam had died and lay buried, and that Jesus set up His trophy over death in the place where death had begun its rule. For He went forth bearing His cross as a trophy in opposition to the tyranny of death, and, as is customary with conquerors, He also carried on His shoulders the symbol of His victory. What matter that the Jews were here acting with an altogether different end in view.

And so He was crucified, and with Him thieves, unwittingly fulfilling prophecy in this detail also. Indeed, the very things which were done to revile Him were the ones that contributed to reveal the truth, in order that you might learn its power. I

Arrival at Golgotha (particular) EL GRECO
Toledo Cathedral

"He went forth bearing His cross as a trophy in opposition
to the tyranny of death. He came to the place called the Skull
and He was crucified."

ST. JOHN CHRYSOSTOM

say this for the Prophet had foretold this circumstance, also, from ancient times in the words: "He was reputed with the wicked."

The Evil Spirit, of course, certainly wished to confuse the issue, but he did not succeed. There were indeed three crucified, but Jesus alone was glorified, that you might learn that it was His power that was in control of everything. Even though it was when the three were fastened to the cross that the miracles took place, no one attributed anything of what took place to any one of the others, but to Jesus only. Thus, the strategy of the devil was foiled. I say this for one of the other two was saved. Not only, then, did He not diminish His glory by the crucifixion, but He even augmented it not a little. For, to convert the thief on the cross and conduct him to paradise was an achievement in no way inferior to that of splitting open the rocks.

"And Pilate also wrote an inscription," at the same time to avenge himself, and even to defend Christ. Pilate set the inscription in place as if it were to serve as a kind of trophy, giving voice to a splendid message. Moreover, he made this clear, not in one tongue only, but in three languages. He did this because Christ was slandered even when He was on the cross.

Now, the soldiers divided His garments among themselves, but not His tunic. Notice how they frequently caused prophecies to be fulfilled by their wicked deeds, for this deed had also been foretold. Furthermore, even though there were three crucified, the prophecy was fulfilled only with reference to Christ. Kindly notice the exactness of the prophecy, too. The prophet declared not only that they divided the garments among themselves, but also that they did not rend them. Thus, the soldiers divided some of Christ's garments into parts, but they did not divide the tunic; on the contrary, they settled its possession by lot.

These things the soldiers did, while He Himself, though crucified, gave His Mother to His disciple's keeping, to instruct us to take care of our parents, even to our last breath. Here, Christ showed great tenderness and gave Mary into the keeping of the disciple whom He loved. But why did He address no other word to John and give him no comfort in His grief? Because it was not the time for words of consolation. Besides, he received the reward for his fidelity in that he was deemed worthy of such an honor as this.

Notice, also, how He did everything with calmness, even though crucified: speaking to the disciple about His mother, fulfilling prophecies, holding out to the thief fair hope for the future. Yet, before being crucified, He was observed to be sweating, in an agony, fearful. Why in the world was this? By no means did this occur by chance, by no means was it without a clear purpose. For, in the previous time, the frailty of His human nature was demonstrated, while here the infinite extent of His power was being shown.

"There were women standing by the cross," and the weaker sex at that time appeared the stronger, so completely were all things turned upside-down for the moment. And when Christ had confided His Mother to the disciple, He said, "Behold thy son." What an honor! With what a great dignity He honored His disciple! He Himself was now departing, so He entrusted her to the disciple to take care of.

"After this Jesus, knowing that all things were accomplished," that is, He knew that no part of the divine plan remained as yet unfulfilled. The Evangelist endeavored in every way to show that this death was something new, if, in fact, every detail was controlled by the One who was dying, and death did not enter His body until He Himself willed it, and He willed it only after all had been fulfilled. That is why He had said, "I have power to lay down my life and I have power to take it up again." Therefore, knowing that all things were now accomplished, He said: "I thirst," in this once again fulfilling a prophecy.

They offered Him a sponge soaked in wine, and "when He had taken it, He said, 'It is consummated!'" All was done calmly and authoritatively. Since all things had been consummated, "Bowing His head, He gave up His spirit," that is, He expired. By all these details, the Evangelist made it clear that Christ Himself is Lord of all.

ST. AMBROSE:

Letters to Priests

And for the rest, consider, dearly beloved, why Jesus suffered outside the gate, and do you leave this earthly city, because your city is Jerusalem which is above. Live there so that you may say, "Our abode is in heaven." Therefore, Jesus went forth from the city so that you, going forth from the world, might be above the world. Moses, the only one to see God, had his tabernacle outside the camp when he spoke with God. The blood of victims, which were offered for sins, was offered on altars, but their bodies were burned outside the camp because no one who is in the midst of the evils of this world can be rid of sin, nor is his blood acceptable to God unless he leaves the defilement of the body.

And Mary, the Mother of the Lord, stood at the cross of her Son, outside the gates of the city. No one told me this except St. John the Evangelist. Others described how the earth was shaken during the Lord's passion, how the sky was covered with darkness, that the sun was darkened, that the thief was received into paradise after his confession of faith. John taught what the others did not, how

Excerpts from the letter to the Church at Vercelli.

202

when He hung on the cross He called His mother by name, thinking it more of import that the Victor over suffering show His Mother the marks of piety than that He give a heavenly gift.

For, if it is a pious work to give pardon to a thief, it is a sign of richer devotion for a mother to be so honored with the affection of her Son. "Behold," He says, "thy son . . . Behold thy mother." Christ made His will from the cross and apportioned the duties of piety between mother and disciple. The Lord made not only a public, but also a private will, and this will of His, John sealed, a worthy witness of so great a Testator—a good testament not of money, but of life eternal, which was written not with ink, but with the Spirit of the living God, who says, "My tongue is the pen of a ready scribe."

Nor was Mary less than was befitting the Mother of Christ. When the Apostles fled, she stood before the cross and with reverent gaze beheld her Son's wounds, for she awaited not her Child's death, but the world's salvation. Or perhaps that "regal chamber" knew that her Son's death would be the world's redemption, and she thought through her own death she would give herself, too, for the common weal. But Jesus had no need of help in the

Redemptive work, for He alone saved all. Therefore He says, "I have become as a man without help, free among the dead."

Imitate Mary, holy mothers, who in her dearly beloved Son set forth such an example of motherly virtue. Mothers, ween your children, love them, but pray for them that they may be long-lived above the earth, not on it, but above it. Nothing is long-lived on this earth, and that which lasts long is brief and more hazardous. Warn them rather to take up the cross of the Lord than to love this life.

ST. AMBROSE:

The Holy Spirit

Christ died according to the flesh. Indeed, He died in that which He took from the Virgin, not in that which He had from the Father, for Christ died in that in which He was crucified. But the Son of God was crucified, who took on flesh and bones, that on the cross the temptations of our flesh might die.

For He took on what He was not, that He might conceal what He was; He concealed what He was, that He might be tempted in it, and that that which He was not might be redeemed, that He might call us to that which He was, through that which He was not.

Oh, the divine mystery of that cross, on which weakness hangs, might is free, vices are fixed, trophies are raised! Therefore a certain saint said, "Pierce thou my flesh with nails from fear of Thee"; not with nails of iron, he says, but of fear and faith; for the bonds of virtue are mightier than those of punishment.

Therefore, crucify sin, that you may die to sin, for he who dies to sin lives to God. You should live

Excerpts from Chapters 9 and 10.

for Him who did not spare His own Son, that in His body He might crucify our passions. For Christ died for us that we might live in His renewed body. Therefore, not our life but our guilt died in Him "who" it is said, "bore our sins in His body upon the tree, that we, being separated from our sins should live with justice, by the wounds of whose stripes we have been healed."

Therefore, that wood of the cross is our conveyance, as it were, the ship of our salvation, not a punishment, for there is no other salvation than the conveyance of eternal salvation. While seeking after death, I do not feel it; while contemning punishment, I do not suffer; while disregarding fear, I do not know it.

Who is it, then, by the wounds of whose stripes we have been healed but Christ our Lord, of whom the same Isaias prophesied that His stripes were our remedy, of whom the Apostle Paul wrote in his Epistles: "He who knew no sin was made sin for us." This indeed was divine in Him, that His flesh did not sin, nor did the creature of the body taken on in Him commit sin. For what wonder is it if the Godhead alone did not sin, since It had no incentives to sin? But if God alone is without sin, surely every creature by its own nature, as we have said, is subject to sin.

Finally, that we may know that this mystery of the common Redemption was very clearly revealed by the prophets, you have it said also in this place: "Behold He has taken away your sins," not because Christ put aside His sins, who did not sin, but because in the flesh of Christ the whole human race was absolved of its sins.

ST. AMBROSE:

Letters to Bishops

Until the price was paid for all men by the shedding of the Lord's blood for the forgiveness of all, blood was required of each man who, by the Law and the customary rite, was following the holy precepts of religion. Since the price has been paid for all after Christ the Lord suffered, there is no longer need for the blood of each individual to be shed by circumcision, for in the blood of Christ the circumcision of all has been solemnized, and in His cross we have all been crucified with Him, and buried together in His tomb, and planted together in the likeness of His death that we may no longer be slaves of sin, "For he who is dead is acquitted of sin."

Some think to find fault with God's judgment for having given the command about the observance of circumcision, or a law directing the shedding of blood; they must also think that the Lord Jesus is at fault for having shed not a little, but a great deal, of blood for the redemption of this world. Even today He bids us shed our blood in the great struggle of religion, saying, "If anyone wishes to come after me, let him take up his cross and follow me."

Excerpts from the letter to Constantius.

If such an accusation is unjust when a man offers himself completely out of love, and cleanses himself by the shedding of much blood (the martyrs), how can we blame the Law for exacting a mere drop of blood, when we preach that the Lord Jesus commands the shedding of much blood, and the death of the whole body?

Neither was the symbol and outward appearance of circumcision useless, by which the people of God, marked with a certain seal of the body, were set off from other nations. But, now that the name of Christ has been given them, they need no bodily sign, for they have attained the honor of a divine title. Why was it absurd for them to seem to bear some pain or labor for piety's sake, that by these difficulties their devotion might be better tried? It is also becoming that from the very cradle of life the symbol of religion should grow with us, and an older person would be ashamed not to meet labor and pain when his tender infancy had overcome them both.

Christian people now have no need of the light pain of circumcision; they bear with them the death of the Lord; in their aspect of baptized men they engrave on their forehead contempt of death, knowing that without the cross of the Lord they cannot be saved. Who would use a needle in battle while armed with stronger weapons?

It was fitting for this partial circumcision of the male to take place before the coming of Him who was to circumcise the whole man, and for the human race to be partially prepared to believe that which is perfect. Just as many kinds of baptism were known of old, because the true sacrament of baptism in spirit and water which would redeem the whole man was to follow, so circumcision of many first had to take place because the circumcision of the Lord's passion was to follow, which Jesus bore like the Lamb of God in order to take away the sins of the world.

Although the law is spiritual, it is clearly manifest even by the letter of the Law that the Gentiles were not bound to observe circumcision. Circumcision was but a sign of the fullness of life to follow. All must be saved through circumcision of the heart, not of a small portion of one member.

The Apology

Consequently there came one whom God had foretold would come to renew and shed light upon that doctrine: it was Christ, the Son of God. It was proclaimed in advance that the Lord and Master of this grace and teaching, the Enlightener and Guide of the human race, would be the Son of God, yet His birth was not such that He must blush at the name of son or the thought of paternal seed. Not as the result of incestuous intercourse with a sister or the violation of a daughter or another's wife has He for His Father a god with horns, nor one who, like the lover of Danae, was turned to gold. Such are the stories which you have attributed to Jupiter; such are your deities.

But the Son of God did no violence to the purity of His mother. Indeed, let us discuss His nature and then the manner of His birth will be understood. When a ray is shot forth from the sun, a part is taken from the whole; but there will be sun in the ray because it is a sun ray; its nature is not separated, but extended. Thus, spirit proceeds from spirit and God from God, just as a light is kindled from light.

Excerpts from Chapter 21.

The source of the substance remains whole and unimpaired, although you may borrow from it many offshoots of its quality.

Thus, too, what proceeds from God is God and the Son of God, and both are one. This ray of God, then, as was ever foretold in the past, descended into a certain virgin and, becoming flesh in her womb, was born as one who is man and God united. The flesh, provided with a soul, is nourished, matures, speaks, teaches, acts, and is Christ.

The Jews knew that Christ would come; in fact, it was to them that He was foretold. For His two comings have been made known in advance. The first has already been fulfilled when He came in the lowliness of human nature. The second is to come at the end of the world in the manifestation of the majesty of His Godhead.

Yet He is rejected by some people since they consider Him merely a man, on the basis of His lowliness. They may esteem Him only as a wonder-worker because of His power, missing the clear manifestation that He is the Word of God. For, with a word He drove evil-spirits from men, gave sight again to the blind, cleansed lepers, healed paralytics, and finally, by a word, restored the dead to life; He reduced to obedience the very elements of nature, calming storms and walking upon the water.

Even His death had been foretold by the prophets, and He Himself predicted it–that He would be betrayed and crucified. And even fastened to the cross, He manifested many signs which distinguished His death. For He anticipated the duty of the executioner and, with a word, of His own accord, He breathed forth His spirit. At the same moment, although the sun was in the midst of her course, the daylight disappeared.

Then He was taken down from the cross and laid in a sepulcher. The place was carefully surrounded with a large band of armed guards, lest— since He had foretold that on the third day He would rise from the dead–His disciples steal away His body and thereby trick them for all their apprehension.

But, lo! on the third day the earth suddenly quaked and the massive stone which blocked the entrance to the sepulcher rolled back. The guards were scattered in fear and, although none of the disciples appeared on the scene, there was nothing to be found in the sepulcher except the winding sheets. Christ spent forty days with some of His disciples in Galilee, a province of Judea, teaching them what they were to teach. Then, when they had been ordained for the office of preaching throughout the world, a cloud enveloped Him and He was taken up into heaven.

The disciples listened to the command of God, their Master, and spread throughout the world, and, after enduring with constancy much suffering from persecution, finally, because of the savage cruelty of Nero, sowed the seed of Christian blood at Rome with joy, through their confidence in the truth.

This, then, is a simple, coherent outline of the history of our founding; we have explained briefly the origin of our religion and of our name in connection with its Founder. We say—and we say openly—and though covered with wounds and blood, we cry out to you, our torturers: "It is God we worship, through Christ. It is through Him and in Him that God wills to be known and worshipped."

ST. HILARY OF POITIERS:

The Trinity

We must now study the nature of the glorification of the Son and whence it comes. I believe that God is unchangeable and that neither defect or improvement, nor gain or loss affect His eternity, but what He is He always is, for this is peculiar to God. That which always is will never have anything in its nature that is compatible with non-being. How, therefore, will He be glorified, since His nature has all that it needs and no decline has set in within Him so that He may not receive anything in Himself nor take back anything that He has lost?

We are embarrassed and we hesitate. The Evangelist does not leave the weakness of our understanding in a quandary, for he shows the glory that the Son will render to the Father when he says: "Even as thou hast given him power over all flesh, in order that to all thou hast given him he may give everlasting life. Now this is everlasting life, that they may know thee, the only true God, and him whom thou hast sent, Jesus Christ."

The glory which the Father receives from the Son consists in this, that He must be perceived by us. The glory was this, that the Son, who had be-

Excerpts from Book 3.

come incarnate, received power from Him over all flesh because He would bestow eternal life upon those who had fallen from grace, who were corporeal, and who were subject to death. Eternal life for us was not a result of an act but of a power, since the glory of eternity is acquired not by a new atonement but by the recognition of God alone. Therefore, the glory of God is not increased, for He has not suffered a loss so that there should be an increase. Through the Son, He is glorified in the midst of us, who are ignorant, fugitives, sinners, hopelessly dead, and surrounded by lawless darkness.

And He is glorified by this, that the Son has received from Him the power over all flesh to which He will give everlasting life. Hence, these words of the Son glorify the Father. As a consequence, when the Son received everything, He was glorified by the Father. On the other hand, the Father is glorified when all things are done through the Son. The glory that has been received is returned in such a manner that whatever glory the Son possesses belongs completely to the glory of the Father, because He has received everything from the Father.

Finally, He tells us in what eternal life consists: "that they may know thee, the only true God, and him whom thou hast sent, Jesus Christ." What difficult questions arise here and what is the nature of the contradiction in terms? It is life to know the true God, but this in itself does not obtain life. What is, therefore, connected with it? "And him whom thou hast sent, Jesus Christ."

Therefore, the Son clearly glorifies the Father in that which follows: "I have glorified thee on earth, since I have accomplished the work that thou hast given me to do." The praise of the Father comes entirely from the Son, because those things for which the Son will be acclaimed will be a commendation of the Father. He fulfills everything that the Father has willed. The Son of God is born as man, but the power of God is manifested at His birth from the Virgin. The Son of God is seen as man, but appears as God in the works of man. The Son of God is nailed to the cross, but on the cross God overcomes the death of man.

Christ, the Son of God, dies, but all flesh is vivified in Christ. The Son of God goes to Limbo, and man is brought back to heaven. The more such things are praised in Christ, the greater will be the approbation of Him from whom Christ as God derives His origin. By such means as these, therefore, does the Father glorify the Son on earth, and again, the Son by the miracles of His power gives glory to Him from whom He comes in the sight of the ignorant and foolish world.

This interchange of glory is certainly not concerned with an increase in the divine nature, but

217

with the honor that He received from those who did not know Him. What did the Father not possess in abundance, He from whom everything comes? Or what was wanting to the Son in whom, as it pleased Him, all the fullness of the Godhead dwelt? Consequently, the Father is glorified on earth because the work which He commanded is accomplished.

Let us see the glory that the Son expects from the Father. In the sentences that follow it is stated: "I have glorified thee on earth, since I have accomplished the work that thou hast given me to do. And now do thou, Father, glorify me with thyself, with the glory I had with thee before the world existed. I have manifested thy name to the men whom thou hast given me." Therefore, the Father has been glorified by the miracles of the Son when He is recognized as God, when He is revealed as the Father of the only-begotten, when for our salvation He even willed that His Son be born as man from the Virgin, and in Him all those things, which began with the birth from the Virgin, are accomplished in the Passion.

Consequently, because the Son of God, perfect in every part that He possesses, and born before all time with the fullness of the Godhead, and, now become man according to the origin of His flesh, was approaching His consummation in death, He prays that He may be glorified with God as He was

Head of the Crucified Christ, Margaritone D'Arezzo
Municipal Gallery, Florence

"The Son of God is nailed to the cross, but on the cross
    God overcomes the death of man."

St. Hilary of Poitiers

glorifying Him on earth, for at that time the powers of God were being glorified in the flesh before a world that did not know Him.

Now, what is the nature of the glory that He expects with the Father? It is that, of course, which He had with Him before the world was made. He had the fullness of the Godhead and still has it, for He is the Son of God. He who was the Son of God also began to be the Son of man, for the Word was made flesh. He did not lose what He was, but began to be what He was not. He did not cease to possess His own nature, but He received what was ours.

He prays that what He had assumed might derive profit from that glory of His which He had never lost. Therefore, since the Son is the Word and the Word was made flesh, and the Word was God and this was in the beginning with God, and the Word was the Son before the foundation of the world, the Son now made flesh prayed that the flesh might begin to be to the Father what the Word was, in order that what belonged in time might receive the splendor of His glory which is timeless, in order that when the corruption of the flesh was transformed it might be assimilated into the power of God and the incorruptibility of the Spirit.

Hence, this is the prayer of God, this the profession of the Son to the Father, this the petition of the flesh in which all see Him on the day of judgment and which they will recognize from the wounds and the cross, in which He was transfigured on the mount, in which He ascended into heaven, in which He sits at the right hand of God, in which He was seen by Paul, in which He was honored by Stephen.

Against Julian

No one is delivered from the wrath of God unless he is reconciled with God through the Mediator, wherefore the Mediator Himself says: "He who is unbelieving towards the Son shall not see life, but the wrath of God rests upon him." He did not say it will come, but "it rests upon him." Therefore, both adults, through their own heart and voice, and infants, through that of another, believe and confess so they may be reconciled to God through the death of His Son, lest the wrath of God rest upon them whom their vitiated origin makes guilty.

The Apostle says: "When as yet we were sinners, Christ died for us. Much more now that we are justified by his blood shall we be saved through him from the wrath. For if when we were enemies we were reconciled to God by the death of His Son, much more, having been reconciled, shall we be saved by his life. And not this only, but we exult also in God, through our Lord Jesus Christ, through whom we have now received reconciliation. Therefore as through one man sin entered into the world and through sin death, and thus death has passed unto all men; in whom all have sinned."

Excerpts from Book 6.

Do not deprive infants of the reconciliation which is made through the death of the Son of God who Himself entered into the world without sin. Do not let the wrath of God rest upon them because of him, Adam, through whom sin entered into the world. But that one sin was enough, which, also, by itself sufficed for condemnation, while grace was not content to destroy only that one, but also all the additional sins, that justification might be made by the remission of all sins. Hence it is said: "The judgment was from one man unto condemnation, but grace is from many offenses unto justification."

For, just as infants do not imitate Christ because they cannot do so, yet can receive His spiritual grace, so without imitating the first man, they are nonetheless bound by contagion from his carnal generation. If you said they are strangers to the sin of the first man because they do not imitate him by their own will, by the same reasoning you estrange them from the justice of Christ because they do not imitate Christ by their own free will.

It is said that through one, sin passed into all, and, later, that through the disobedience of one, many were constituted sinners. In like manner, when it is said: "By the obedience of the one many will be constituted just," none is excepted. We must understand that those who are many are all—not because all men are justified in Christ, but because all who are justified can be justified in no other way than in Christ. We can say, for instance, that all men enter a certain house through one door, not because all men do enter that house, but because no one enters except through that door.

All, then, are unto death through Adam; all unto life through Christ. "As in Adam all die, so in Christ all will be made to live." That is to say, from the first origin of the human race, none is unto death except through Adam, and through Adam none is unto anything but death. And, none is unto life except through Christ, and through Christ none is unto anything but life.

If some are saved without Christ, then some are also justified without Christ; therefore Christ died in vain. For there must have been another way—in nature, in free choice, in the law, natural or written, by which they who so wished could be saved and be just. Who but the unjust would bar these other just images of God from the kingdom of God? Perhaps you will say it is accomplished more easily through Christ? Could you not also say this of the Law—that there is justice through the Law, but more easily through Christ? Yet the Apostle says: "If justice be by the Law, then Christ died in vain."

Therefore, besides the one Mediator of God and men, the man Christ Jesus, there is no other name under heaven whereby we must be saved.

For this reason it is said: "In Christ all shall be made alive," because in Him, God has defined the faith for all, raising Him from the death. In the new covenant through the blood of the Mediator, the paternal debt having been cancelled, man by rebirth begins to be no longer subject to the paternal debts that bind him at birth, as the Mediator Himself says: "And call no one on earth your father," inasmuch as we find another birth by which we shall not succeed our father, but shall live forever with the Father.

Therefore the Patriarchs remind us: Sacrifices for sins were offered even for new-born infants; and: Not even an infant of one day upon the earth is clean of sin. In sum, the Apostle says: "All we who have been baptized into Christ Jesus have been baptized into his death, so that we are dead to sin, but alive to God in Christ Jesus."

PRUDENTIUS:

Hymns

Great Moses in a former age
Escaped proud Pharao's foolish law,
And as the savior of his race
Prefigured Christ who was to come.

A cruel edict had been passed
Forbidding Hebrew mothers all,
When sons were born to them, to rear
These virile pledges of their love.

Devoutly scornful of the king,
A zealous midwife found a way
To hide her charge and keep him safe
For future glory and renown.

And when the boy to manhood grew,
God chose him as His own high priest,
Through whose pure hands He might transmit
His law engraved on slabs of stone.

In this great man may we not see
A figure of our Savior, Christ?
By slaying the Egyptian lord,
That leader lifted Israel's yoke;

Excerpts from *A Hymn for Epiphany.*

But when beneath the yoke of sin
We bow in ceaseless servitude,
Our Captain wounds the enemy
And frees us from the shades of Death.

And Moses cheers with waters sweet
His people ransomed in the sea,
When led by him through cleansing flood
And guided by the pillar's light.

While Israel's hosts in battle join,
He overwhelms fierce Amalec
By lifting up his arms on high,
Prefiguring then the cross of Christ.

A truer prototype of Christ was
Josue, who led his tribes
With untold cost and sacrifice,
Victorious, to the promised lands.

Also, twelve stones from Jordan's bed,
Left dry when waters backward flowed,
He raised and firmly set in place,
The type of Christ's Apostles twelve.

Then rightly do the Magi hold
That they have seen Judea's King,
For all the deeds of ancient chiefs
In figure told of Christ the Lord.

Of Judges who in olden times
Ruled Jacob's race, He is the King;

King now of holy mother Church,
Of both the temples, new and old.

The sons of Ephraim worship Him,
With all Manasses' holy house,
And tribes sprung from the brothers twelve
All honor Him as Lord and God.

Nay, even children of lost tribes,
Who followed false and shameful rites,
And all who shaped in fiery forge
The forms of Baal to adore,

Forsake their fathers' gloomy gods
Of metal, wood, and senseless stone;
Leave idols, hewn and carved by man,
To worship Christ in spirit and truth.

Rejoice, all nations of the earth,
Judea, Egypt, Greece and Rome,
With Scythia, Thrace, and Persian realms:
Now over all one King holds sway.

Then praise your Lord, you that rejoice,
And all by desolation tried,
In health, affliction or decay:
For none shall taste eternal death!

Chapter 7

ALLELUIA!

"It is true, I come quickly!"
Amen! Come, Lord Jesus! The
grace of our Lord Jesus Christ
be with all. Amen.

Apocalypse 22:20-21

The Alleluia of Easter is the cry of Christian faith, the testimony to our belief in the Resurrection of Our Lord, the great proof of His divinity. It should endure through all the days of our life, until we graduate, through death, into the choirs of heaven, until we can join in the eternal praise of God with the joyful "Holy, Holy, Holy!"

For ours is a life of hope. Relying on the infinite goodness and mercy of God, we hope to obtain the pardon of our sins, the help of grace, and life everlasting. Even in the midst of this vale of tears, the Christian is by vocation an optimist. He knows that at any moment God can say "Enough," and step in and help him. He knows that his prayers ascend to a heavenly Father, who cares for him.

Even death is a triumph for the Christian. It is a time of "going home," of eternal rest, of accepting the place in the kingdom prepared for those who love Christ. Of course there is the fear of having offended the Beloved, but not the servile fear that terrifies worldlings. With St. Paul, we know Him in whom we have believed; we have lived with Christ living in us. We can exult like a giant, to run the course, and cry out with tremendous longing: "Come, Lord Jesus. Come!"

ST. AUGUSTINE:

The City of God

Even if we should grant that the resurrection of the body was once beyond belief, the fact is that the whole world now believes that the earthly body of Christ has been taken up to heaven. Learned and unlearned alike no longer doubt the resurrection of His flesh and His ascension into heaven, while there is but a handful who continue to be puzzled. Now, what all these believers believed was either credible or not. If it was credible, then the incredulous should ask themselves whether they are not rather ridiculous. If it was not credible and yet was believed, then we have something really incredible, namely that something incredible should be so universally believed.

We have then two incredibles: one, the resurrection of any body in eternal life; the other, the world's belief in this incredibility. But notice. The same God predicted both before the event. Now, one of these incredibilities has become a fact before our very eyes, namely, the incredibility of the world believing something incredible. Why, then, should we doubt that the other will be fulfilled, namely, that the incredible truth will also come to pass.

Excerpts from Book 22.

What is really hard to believe, for anyone who stops to think about it, is the way the world came to believe. The fisherman whom Christ sent with the nets of faith into the sea of the world were men unschooled in the liberal arts and utterly untrained as far as education goes, men with no skill in the use of language, armed with no weapons of debate, plumed with no rhetorical power. Yet, the catch this handful of fishermen took was enormous and marvelous. They hauled in fish of every sort, not excluding those rare specimens, the philosophers themselves.

We may add, then, if you please, this third incredibility to the other two; in fact, it must be added whether one likes it or not, simply because there are three incredibilities which actually occurred. It is incredible that Christ should have risen in the flesh, and with His flesh have ascended into heaven; it is incredible that the world should have believed such a thing; it is incredible that men so rude and lowly, so few and unaccomplished, should have convinced the world, including men of learning, of something so incredible and have convinced men so conclusively.

It is no less a fact that the Resurrection of Christ and His Ascension into heaven, with the flesh in which He rose, is now preached to the whole world and is believed. Of course, the whole world could believe without a miracle if a multitude of senators, imperial courtiers, and famous scholars had declared that they had seen the Ascension and then took pains to publicize the fact, but the truth is that the world has believed a handful of unknown and unlearned nobodies who said and wrote that they had seen the miracle.

The world has believed this insignificant group of lowly, unimportant, and uneducated men precisely because the divine character of what happened is more marvelously apparent in the insignificance of such witnesses. What gave power to the preachers who persuaded the world was not the eloquence of the words they uttered, but the miracles in the deeds they did.

Those who had not themselves seen Christ rising from the dead and ascending into heaven with His flesh believed the men who said they had seen the miracle, not merely because these men said so, but also because these men themselves worked miracles. For example, many people were astonished to hear these men, who knew but two languages (and in some cases, only one) suddenly break forth into so many tongues that everybody in the audience understood.

They saw a man who had been lame from earliest infancy now, after forty years, stand upright at a word uttered by these witnesses who spoke in the name of Christ. Pieces of cloth that touched their bodies were found to heal the sick. Uncounted people suffering from various diseases set themselves in line in the streets where the Apostles were to pass and where their shadows would fall upon the sick, and many of these people were at once restored to health. Besides many other marvels wrought in the name of Christ, there were even cases of men restored to life.

In such a period how could possibilities so counter to experience as the Resurrection of Christ's flesh and His Ascension into heaven have found entrance into men's ears and hearts and minds, unless the possibility had been realized in fact, and a proof had been found in the divinity of the fact involved, namely, the fact of the divinity, not to mention the corroboration of manifest miracles? The fact is that, in spite of the terrors and attacks inspired by a series of fierce persecutions, not only was the Resurrection of Christ loyally believed and fearlessly proclaimed, but also the resurrection and immortality of the bodies of His followers in the world to come.

And the seeds of this hope scattered throughout the world were watered by the blood of martyrs. Not only did men read the earlier prophecies of these future realities, but they saw the miracles that occurred, and were soon convinced that the reality, new as it was to experience, was not counter to reason. The result was that the truth that the world once rejected with all the fury of hate it now sought with the fervor of faith.

ST. PETER CHRYSOLOGUS:

Christ's Resurrection

Dearly beloved, today we shall consider the Lord's resurrection. In relation to this, if Christ's birth from the Virgin is something divine, how much more so is His resurrection from the dead! Therefore, let not that which is divine be heard with merely human interpretation.

"Late in the night of the Sabbath," Scripture says, "as it began to dawn towards the first day of the week." The evening of the Sabbath—for the world, evening terminates the day; it does not begin it. The evening fades into darkness; it does not grow bright. It does not change into dawn because it does not know the sunrise.

Evening, the mother of night, gives birth to daylight! It changes the customary order while it acknowledges its Creator. It displays a new symbolic mystery. It is eager to serve its Creator rather than the march of time.

"Late in the night of the Sabbath," we read, "as it began to dawn towards the first day of the week, Mary Magdalen and the other Mary came to see the sepulchre." Earlier, a woman hastened to sin; now,

Excerpts from Sermon 74.

later on, a woman hastens to repentance. In the morning a woman knew that she had corrupted Adam; in the evening a woman seeks Christ.

"Mary Magdalen and the other Mary came to see the sepulchre." A woman had drawn a beginning of perfidy out of Paradise; now a woman hastens to draw faith from the sepulcher. She who had snatched death out of life now hurries to get life out of death.

"Mary came." This is the name of Christ's Mother. Therefore, the one who hastened was a mother in name. She came as a woman, that woman who had become the mother of those who die, might become the mother of the living, and fulfillment might be had in the Scriptural statement about her: "that is, the mother of all the living."

"Mary came, and also the other Mary." Scripture does not say *they* came, but *she* came. Two women of one name came through a symbolic mystery, not through chance. "Mary came, and also the other Mary." She came, but another, too. Another came, but the first, too, so that woman might be changed in life, but not in name; in virtue, but not in sex. A woman had been the intermediary of the fall and ruin, and a woman was to be the one to announce the Resurrection.

"Mary came to the sepulchre." The sight of the tree had deceived her; the sight of the sepulcher was to restore her. A guileful glance had laid her low; a saving glance was to raise her up again.

"And behold," the Gospel continues, "there was a great earthquake; for an angel of the Lord came down from heaven." The earth trembled, not because an angel came down from heaven, but because its Ruler ascended from hell. "And behold, there was a great earthquake." The heart of the earth is stirred. The depths of the earth leap up. The earth trembles, the huge mountains quiver, the foundations of the earth are battered. Hell is caught and set in its place. Death gets judged—death which, rushing against guilty men, runs into its Judge; death which after long domination over its slaves rose up against its Master; death which waxed fierce against men but encountered God.

Rightly, therefore, did the rule of hell perish, and its laws get blotted out. The power of death was taken away, and in penalty for its rashness in attempting to harm its Judge, death brought the dead back to life. Thereupon, bodies were yielded up. The man was put back together, and his life was restored, and now everything holds together through forgiveness, because the condemnation has passed over on to the Author of life.

"And behold, there was a great earthquake." Now there was a great earthquake. Oh, if at that other time even some light whirlwind had blown down that death-bearing tree! Oh, if some smoke-like cloud had darkened that woman's vision! Oh, if a dark cloud had enveloped the beauty of that deathly fruit! Oh, if the hand had trembled upon touching the forbidden fruit! However, allurements always promote vices and sweet things induce sins, but austere and manly pursuits promote virtues.

"For an angel of the Lord came down from heaven." Through the Resurrection of Christ and the defeat of death, men once more entered into relationship with heaven. Moreover, woman, who had entered into a deadly plan with the devil, now enjoyed a life-giving conversation with the angel.

"For an angel of the Lord came down from heaven and rolled back the stone." Scripture did not say *rolled,* but *rolled back* the stone. When rolled forward it was a proof of His death. When rolled back, it was proof of His Resurrection. Blessed is the stone which could both conceal Christ and reveal Him! Blessed the stone which opens hearts no less than the sepulcher! Blessed is the stone which produces faith in the Resurrection, and a resurrection of faith; which is a proof that God's body has arisen! Here the order of things is changed. Here, the sepulcher swallows death, not a dead man. The abode of death becomes a life-giving dwelling. A new kind of womb conceives one who is dead and brings Him forth alive!

"For an angel of the Lord came down from heaven and drawing near rolled back the stone and sat upon it!" An angel does not weary. Then why did he sit? He was sitting as a doctor of faith and a teacher of the Resurrection. He was sitting upon a rock, that its very solidity might impart firmness to those who believe. The angel was placing the foundations of faith upon the rock, on which Christ was going to build His Church, as He said: "Thou art Peter, and upon this rock I will build My Church."

"His countenance was like lightning," the Gospel says, "and his raiment like snow." Is not brilliance of lightning enough for an angel? What did raiment add to heavenly nature? But by such splendor he foreshadowed the beauty and pattern of our resurrection. For those who arise in Christ are transformed with the glory of Christ.

The Three Marys at the Tomb, Duccio
Museum dell'Opera del Duomo, Siena

" 'For an angel of the Lord came down from heaven and drawing near rolled back the stone and sat upon it!' He was sitting as a doctor of faith and a teacher of the Resurrection."

ST. PETER CHRYSOLOGUS

ST. CLEMENT OF ROME:

Second Letter to the Corinthians

Brothers, we must think of Jesus Christ as of God—as the "judge of the living and the dead." And we must not think lightly of our Savior. For in thinking lightly of Him, we also hope to receive but little. And we sin, those of us who listen as if to an unimportant matter, not knowing whence, by whom, and to what place we have been called, and how much suffering Jesus Christ endured for our sakes.

What return, then, shall we make to Him, or what fruit worthy of that which He has given us? How much devotion do we owe Him! He has lavished the light upon us; He has spoken to us as a father to his sons; He has saved us when we were perishing. What praise, then, shall we give to Him, or what payment in return for what we have received?

Blinded in our understanding, we bowed down to sticks and stones and gold and silver and brass, the works of men; and our whole life was nothing else but death. While we were covered with dark-

Excerpts from chapters 1, 3, and 4. This homily comes from the first centuries of Christianity. Its author is not known definitely; it may be from Pope St. Soter. It was preserved with St. Clement's *Letter* and so has received this title.

ness and our sight was obscured by this mist, by His will we recovered our sight, putting off the cloud which invested us. For He had mercy on us and, out of pity, saved us, seeing in us much waywardness and destruction and no hope of salvation except such as might come from Him. For He called us when we were not, and out of nothing willed us to be.

Since, then, He has bestowed such mercy on us, first that we the living do not sacrifice to gods who are dead nor worship them, but through Him know the Father of Truth—what is true knowledge concerning Him except not to deny Him through whom we knew the Father?

He Himself says, "He who confesses me before men, I will confess him before my Father." This, then, is our reward, if we confess Him through whom we were saved. But how do we confess Him? By doing what He says, and not disobeying His commandments, and honoring Him not only with our lips but "with all our heart and all our mind." And He says also in Isaias: "This people honors me with their lips, but their heart is far from me."

Let us not merely call Him Lord, then, for this will not save us. For He says, "Not everyone who says to me 'Lord, Lord' shall be saved, but he who works justice." So then, brothers, let us confess Him in our works by loving one another, by not committing adultery, nor speaking against one another, by not being envious, but by being self-controlled, kindly, good. And we ought to sympathize with one another and not be avaricious. By these works we confess Him, and not by the contrary.

ST. AUGUSTINE:

Faith and Works

But, they argue, in the Acts of the Apostles, on the occasion of the conversion of the 3,000 who, having heard the word, were baptized in one day, Peter preached to them faith alone, by which they believed in Christ. When they had asked: "What shall we do?" Peter answered: "Repent and be baptized every one of you in the name of Jesus Christ for the forgiveness of your sins; and you will receive the gift of the Holy Spirit." Why do they not notice that he said: "Repent"? That meant the stripping off of the old life so that those who are being baptized may put on the new. Of what avail is repentance for dead works if one persists in sin?

To this they answer: Peter wanted them to repent only for their lack of faith in not believing in Christ. Strange presumption if after the expression 'repent' has been heard it indicates an act of infidelity, when the evangelical teaching on the necessity of changing the old way of life for the new has been continuously handed down. What, indeed, is the meaning of what the Apostle puts in this way:

Excerpts from chapters 8-10.

"He who was wont to steal, let him steal no longer," and similar expressions which indicate how to put off the old man and put on the new?

The eunuch, they insist, whom Philip baptized, said nothing more than "I believe Jesus Christ to be the Son of God," and immediately after this profession of faith he was baptized. Does it really seem right that upon simply making this response men should be straightway baptized? Is nothing to be said by the catechist, nothing to be professed by the believer about the Holy Spirit, about holy Church, nothing about the forgiveness of sins, the resurrection of the dead, nothing, finally, about the Lord Jesus Christ Himself except that He is the Son of God—nothing about His Incarnation in the womb of a virgin, His passion, His death on the cross, His burial, His resurrection on the third day, His ascension and sitting at the right hand of the Father?

When the eunuch answered: "I believe Jesus Christ to be the Son of God," if this was enough for him to say in order to go right down into the waters of baptism, why do we not follow his example? Why not imitate it and do away with all the rest of the preparation that we consider so necessary, even when the time for baptism is short and urgent? If, however, Scripture is silent and dismisses the rest of what Philip talked over with the eunuch as understood and taken for granted, the words "Philip baptized him" imply that everything was fulfilled which, for the sake of brevity, may be passed over in Scripture, but which, nevertheless, we know from the unbroken chain of tradition must have been carried out.

Likewise, where it says that Philip preached the Lord Jesus to the eunuch, there must be no doubt that the ensuing catechism embraced all the necessary instruction on the duties and proper mode of living for one who believes in the Lord Jesus. To preach Christ consists in declaring not only what must be believed about Him, but also the precepts that must be observed by one hoping for membership in the unity of the Body of Christ.

Indeed, to preach Christ is to state everything that must be believed about Christ, not only whose Son He is, whence begotten according to His divinity, whence according to His flesh, what He suffered and why He suffered, what is the virtue of His resurrection, what gift of the Spirit He promised and gave to the faithful; but also what kind of members He, the Head, seeks, ordains, loves, frees from the bonds of sin, and leads to eternal life and glory. When these facts are related, sometimes more briefly and with restriction, other times more comprehensively and in greater detail, Christ is being preached. At the same time, what pertains to the habits and morals of the faithful as well as what pertains to faith is not left unsaid.

This point of view is again easily perceived in how they quote from the Apostle Paul, as if, "For I determined not to know anything among you, except Jesus Christ and Him crucified" could possibly mean that nothing else had been taught the Corinthians except what induced belief in Christ in order that they might first be baptized and later be presented a pattern for living. That, they hold, was all the Apostle required of them; yet he said "although they had ten thousand tutors in Christ they had not many fathers" because he himself had begotten them "in Christ Jesus through the gospel."

If, then, he who begot them through the Gospel taught them nothing more than Christ crucified, what if someone should say that they had not heard that Christ had risen from the dead, when they were begotten through the Gospel? How could he say to them: "I delivered to you first of all what I also received, that Christ died for our sins according to the Scriptures, and that he was buried, that he rose again the third day, according to the Scriptures," if he had taught them nothing but the crucifixion?

If they are persistent in their misunderstanding and claim that all this is part of the teaching of

Christ crucified, may they know that there is, indeed, a great deal to learn in Christ crucified and, above all, that our "old self has been crucified with him, in order that the body of sin may be destroyed, that we may no longer be slaves to sin." And again, "But as for me, God forbid that I should glory save in the cross of our Lord Jesus Christ, through whom the world is crucified to me, and I to the world."

Let them attend carefully and see how Christ crucified is taught and learned. Let them see how it is a part of His cross that we, too, be crucified to the world in His Body.

ST. GREGORY THE GREAT:

Dialogues

In the Gospel our Lord says, "Finish your journey while you still have the light." And in the words of the prophet He declares, "In an acceptable time I have heard thee, and in the day of salvation I have helped thee." St. Paul's comment on this is: "And here is the time of pardon; the day of salvation has come already." Solomon, too, says, "Anything you can turn your hand to, do with what power you have; for there will be no work, nor reason, nor knowledge nor wisdom in the nether world where you are going." And David adds, "For his mercy endures forever."

From these quotations it is clear that each one will be presented to the Judge exactly as he was when he departed this life. Yet, there must be a cleansing fire before judgment, because of some minor faults that may remain to be purged away. Does not Christ, the Truth, say that if anyone blasphemes against the Holy Spirit he shall not be forgiven "either in this world or in the world to come"? From this statement we learn that some sins can be forgiven in this world and some in the world to

Excerpts from the fourth dialogue.

come. For, if forgiveness is refused for a particular sin, we must conclude logically that it is granted for others.

This must apply, as I said, to slight transgressions, such as persistent idle talking, immoderate laughter, or blame in the care of property, which can scarcely be administered without fault even by those who know the faults to be avoided, or errors due to ignorance in matters of no great importance. All these faults are troublesome for the soul after death if they are not forgiven while one is still alive. For, when St. Paul says that Christ is the foundation, he adds: "But on this foundation different men will build in gold, silver, precious stones, wood, grass or straw ... and fire will test the quality of each man's workmanship. He will receive a reward, if the building he had added on stands firm! If it is burnt up, he will be the loser; and yet he himself will be saved, though only as men are saved by passing through fire."

Although this may be taken to signify the fire of suffering we experience in this life, it may also refer to the cleansing fire of the world to come, and, if one accepts it in this sense, one must weigh St. Paul's words carefully. When he says that men are saved by passing through fire, he is not referring to men who build on this foundation in iron, bronze or lead, that is, in mortal sins which are indestructible by fire.

He specifies those who build on this foundation in wood, grass and straw, that is, in venial or trivial sins which fire consumes easily. In this connection, we should also remember that in the world to come no one will be cleansed even of the slightest faults, unless he has merited such a cleansing through good works performed in this life. The Holy Sacrifice of Christ, our saving Victim, brings great benefits to souls even after death, provided their sins can be pardoned in the life to come. It is for this reason that Masses are offered for them.

I believe that in some instances miracles were openly performed for living persons who were unaware of the source of their benefits, in order that all those who offer the Holy Sacrifice, without adverting to its efficacy, might come to understand that deceased persons, too, can be absolved from sins through the Mass, provided their sins are pardonable. But remember, the benefits of the Holy Sacrifice are only for those who by good lives have merited the grace of receiving help from the good deeds others perform in their behalf.

The safer course, naturally, is to do for ourselves during life what we hope others will do for us after death. It is better to make one's exit a free man than to seek liberty after one is in chains. We should, therefore, despise this world with all our hearts as though its glory were already spent, and offer our sacrifice of tears to God each day as we immolate His sacred Flesh and Blood.

This Sacrifice alone has the power of saving the soul from eternal death, for it presents to us mystically the death of the Only-begotten Son. Though He is now risen from the dead and dies no more, and "death has no more power over Him," yet, living in Himself immortal and incorruptible, He is again immolated for us in the mystery of the Holy Sacrifice. Where His Body is eaten, there His Flesh is distributed among the people for their salvation.

See, then, how august the Sacrifice is that is offered for us, ever reproducing in itself the passion of the Only-begotten Son for the remission of our sins. For who of the faithful can have any doubt that at the moment of the immolation, at the sound of the priest's voice, the heavens stand open and choirs of angels are present at the mystery of Jesus Christ. There at the altar the lowliest is united with the most sublime, earth is joined to heaven, the visible and invisible somehow merge into one.

ST. AUGUSTINE:

The Creed

Believe: "He ascended into heaven." Believe: He "sitteth at the right hand of the Father." Understand that to sit here means to dwell in the same sense that we say of anyone: he has lived in that country for three years. Christ dwells on the right hand of God the Father; He is there.

"From thence He shall come to judge the living and the dead": the living, those who are still alive; the dead, those who have gone before. It can be interpreted in this way, too: The living are the just; the dead the unjust. He judges both, giving each his due. To the just He will say in judgment: "Come, blessed of my Father, take possession of the kingdom prepared for you from the foundation of the world." Prepare yourselves for this, hope for these blessings; for this live, and so live with this before you, for this believe, for this be baptized, that to you may be said: "Come, blessed of my Father, take possession of the kingdom prepared for you from the foundation of the world." What does He say to those on His left? "Go into everlasting fire which was prepared for the devil and his angels." Thus will Christ judge the living and the dead.

Excerpts from Chapters 4-9.

We have spoken of the first nativity of Christ, without time; we have spoken of the other nativity, in the fullness of time, the nativity of Christ from a virgin; we have spoken of the Passion of Christ; and we have spoken of the judgment of Christ. Everything has been said which had to be said about Christ, the only Son of God, our Lord; but not yet is the Trinity completed. The Creed continues: "And in the Holy Spirit." This Trinity is one God, one nature, one substance, one power, supreme equality, no division, no diversity, perpetual charity. Be baptized and you will be His temple. The Apostle says: "Or do you not know that your members are the temple of the Holy Spirit, who is in you, whom you have from God."

After the praise of the Trinity comes "the holy Church." God and His temple have been pointed out. "For holy is the temple of God," says the Apostle, "and this temple you are." This is holy Church, the one Church, the true Church, the Catholic Church, fighting against all heresies; she can fight, but she cannot be conquered. All heresies are expelled from her as if they were dead branches pruned from the vine; she herself, however, remains fixed in her root, in her vine, in her charity. The gates of hell shall not prevail against her.

"The forgiveness of sins." You have the creed in its perfection in you when you receive baptism.

Let no one say, "I have committed that sin, perhaps it is not forgiven me." What have you done? How great a sin have you committed? Tell me anything terrible that you have done, something serious, horrible, something that makes you shudder just to think about it; whatever you might have done, did you kill Christ? There is nothing worse than that crime, because there is nothing better than Christ. Yet, even that sin was forgiven.

When you have been baptized, hold to the good life in the commandments of God that you may preserve your baptism up to the very end. I do not say to you that you will live here without sin, but they are venial sins which we cannot avoid in this life. Baptism was devised for all sins; for slight sins, without which it is impossible to live, prayer was found. How does the prayer go? "And forgive us our debts, as we also forgive our debtors."

We are cleansed but once by baptism; daily we are cleansed by prayer. But do not commit those sins that compel your separation from the Body of Christ; God forbid that you should! They whom you see doing public penance have committed crimes, either adultery, or some other outrage; that is the reason for the public penance. If their sins were slight, daily prayer would be enough. Within the Church, sins are forgiven in three ways: by baptism, by prayer, and by the greater humility of penance.

We believe also in "the resurrection of the body" which has gone before us in Christ, and the body which has gone before us in the Head awaits resurrection. Christ is the Head of the Church, the Church is the Body of Christ. Our Head has arisen from the dead, has ascended into heaven; where the Head is, there, too, are the members. How, then, do we accept the resurrection of the body? Let no one by any chance think it the same as the resurrection of Lazarus. That you may know that it is not the same, the words "unto life everlasting" are added.

May God regenerate; may God preserve and watch over you; may God bring you unto Himself who is Life Everlasting. Amen.

ST. AMBROSE:

Letters to Laymen

Let us abide there and remain in Him of whom Isaias says, "How beautiful are the feet of those who preach peace and preach good tidings!" Who are those who preach except Peter, Paul and all the Apostles? What do they preach to us except the Lord Jesus?

He is our peace, He is our highest Good, for He is the Good from Good, and from a good tree is gathered good fruit. Then, too, His spirit is good, that Spirit which receives the servants of God from Him and brings them into the right way. Let no one who has the Spirit of God in him deny that He is good, since He Himself says, "Is thy eye evil because I am good?" May there come into our soul, into our innermost heart, this Good which the kind God gives to those who ask Him. Christ is our treasure; He is our way; He is our Wisdom, our righteousness, our Shepherd and the Good Shepherd; He is our Life. See the number of good things in the one Good!

The Evangelists preach these good things to us. David in search of these good things said, "Who will show us good things?" And he shows that the

Excerpts from the letter to Irenaeus.

The Resurrection (particular), EL GRECO
Prado Gallery, Madrid

"Christ is our treasure; He is our way; He is our Wisdom,
our righteousness, our shepherd and the Good Shepherd;
He is our Life. See the number of good things in the one Good!"

ST. AMBROSE

Lord Himself is our Good, saying, "The light of thy countenance is signed upon us." Who is the light of the Father's countenance except the brightness of His glory, the image of the invisible God, in whom the Father is both seen and glorified, as He also glorifies His Son?

The Lord Jesus Himself, therefore, is the Highest Good whom the prophets announced, the angels made known, the Father promised and the Apostles preached. He Himself was the first to preach good tidings to us and said, "I myself who spoke am here"; that is, I who spoke in the prophets, I am present in the body which I took of a virgin; I am present, the inward likeness of God, the express image of His person; and I am present as man. But who knows me?

They saw a man, yet they believed that His works were greater than man. Was it not as man that He wept for Lazarus, and greater than man that He raised him from the dead? Again, was it not as man that He was scourged, and greater than man that He took away the sins of all the world?

Let us hurry to Him in whom that Supreme Good is, since He is Goodness itself. He is the patience of Israel calling you to penance, so you will not come to judgment but may receive the remission of sin. "Do penance," He says. He is the one of whom the prophet Amos cries, "Seek ye good." Christ is the Highest Good, for He needs nothing and abounds in all things. Well may He abound, for in Him dwells bodily the fullness of divinity. Well may He abound, of whose fullness we have all received and in whom we have been filled, as the Evangelist says.

If the soul, with its capacity for pleasure and delight, has tasted this true and Supreme Good and has adhered to both with the means at its disposal, putting away sorrow and fear, then it is wonderfully inflamed. Having embraced the Word of God, the soul knows no bounds, knows no satiety, and says, "Thou art sweet, O Lord, and in thy joy teach me thy laws." Having embraced the Word of God, the soul desires Him above every beauty, loves Him above every joy, is delighted with Him above every pleasure.

The soul presses forward for a glimpse of hidden mysteries, to the very abode of the Word, to the very dwelling place of the Supreme Good, and His light and brightness. In the secret dwelling place of the Father it hastens to hear His words, and having heard them, it finds them sweeter than all things. Let the prophet who has tasted this sweetness teach you, when he says, "How sweet are thy words to my lips, above the honeycomb to my mouth." What else can a soul desire once it has tasted the sweetness of the Word, and seen its brightness?

When Moses remained on the mountain forty days to receive the Law, he had no need of food for the body. Elias, going to that rest, asked that his soul be taken away from him. Even Peter himself, foreseeing on the mountain the glory of the Lord's Resurrection, did not wish to come down, and said, "Lord, it is good for us to be here." How great is the glory of the Divine Essence, how great the graces of the Word at which even angels wish to gaze!

The soul which beholds the Highest Good needs not the body, and, knowing that it should have very little familiarity with it, shuns the world, withdraws from the chains of the flesh, and casts off all bonds of earthly pleasure. Thus Stephen beheld Jesus and had no fear of being stoned to death; in fact, while he was being stoned he prayed, not for himself, but for those by whom he was being murdered. Paul, too, caught up into the third heaven, did not know whether he was in the body or out of it; caught, I say, into paradise, he no longer had need of the body, and after hearing the word of God he was ashamed to descend to the infirmities of the body.

Therefore, let the soul which wishes to approach God raise itself from the body and cling always to that Highest Good which is divine, and lasts forever, and which was from the beginning and which was with God, that is, the Word of God. This is the Divine Being in which we live, and are, and move. This was in the beginning, this is, "The Son of God, Jesus Christ in you," says St. Paul, "in whom there was not Yes and No but only Yes." He Himself told Moses to say, *He Who Is* hath sent me.

ST. AUGUSTINE:

On the Trinity

We have by this time become familiar with the rule according to which the sayings of Scripture about the Son of God are to be understood. And, therefore, we are able to distinguish what sounds in them according to the form of God in which He is equal to the Father, and what sounds in them according to the form of a slave which He assumed, and in which He is less than the Father. Thus we shall no longer be surprised by sentences in the sacred books that apparently conflict with and contradict one another.

For according to the form of God, the Son and the Holy Spirit are equal to the Father, because neither of them is a creature as we have already shown, but according to the form of a slave, a man, He is less than the Father, because He Himself has said: "The Father is greater than I"; He is less than Himself because it was said of Him: "He emptied Himself"; He is less than the Holy Spirit because He Himself declared: "Whoever shall speak blasphemies against the Son of Man, it shall be forgiven him; but whoever shall speak against the Holy Spirit, it shall not be forgiven him."

Excerpts from Book 1.

And He tells us that in the Holy Spirit He did wonderful things: "If I cast out devils in the Spirit of God, then certainly the Kingdom of God has come upon you." And He says in Isaias, in the lesson which He Himself recited in the synagogue, and showed Himself, without any scruple of doubt, that it had been fulfilled in Himself: "The Spirit of the Lord is upon me," He said, "because he has anointed me, to bring good news to the poor he has sent me, to proclaim to the captives release." For these works was He, therefore, sent, as He says, because the Spirit of the Lord was upon Him.

According to the form of God, all things were made through Him. According to the form of a slave, He Himself was made from a woman, made under the Law. According to the form of God, He Himself and the Father are one. According to the form of a slave, He has come not to do His own will but the will of Him who sent Him. According to the form of God, "as the Father has life in himself, so He has given to the Son also to have life in himself." According to the form of a slave "his soul is sorrowful even unto death," and "Father, if it be possible let this cup pass away from me." According to the form of God "He is the true God and eternal life." According to the form of a slave "He became obedient to death, even to the death of the cross."

According to the form of God everything that the Father has is His; and: "All things that are mine are thine, and thine are mine." According to the form of a slave His doctrine is not His, but that of Him who sent Him, and "Of that day or hour no one knows, neither the angels in heaven, nor the Son, but the Father only." According to the form of God it was said: "Before all the hills he has begotten me," that is, before all the most exalted creatures, and: "Before the morning star I have begotten thee," that is, before all the ages and temporal things.

But according to the form of a slave it was said: "The Lord created me in the beginning of his ways." Because according to the form of God He said: "I am the truth," and according to the form of a slave: "I am the way." For since He Himself "the firstborn of the dead" has laid out the road for His Church to the Kingdom of God, to eternal life, of which He is the head even to the extent of giving immortality to the body, He was, therefore, created in the beginning of the ways of God for His works.

For according to the form of God He is "the beginning who also speaks unto us," in which beginning God "made the heavens and the earth," but according to the form of a slave He is "the bridegroom coming out of his chamber." According to the form of God He is the "firstborn of every creature, and he himself is before all creatures, and in Him all things hold together," and according to the form of a slave He is "the head of the body, the Church." According to the form of God He is the Lord of glory, wherefore it is evident that He Himself glorifies His saints. "For those whom he has predestined, them he has also called; and those whom he has called, them he has also justified; and those whom he has justified, them he has also glorified."

For of Him it has been said that He justifies the impious; of Him it has been said that He is just and that He justifies. If, therefore, He has also glorified those whom He has justified, it is He Himself who justifies and glorifies, who is, as I have said, the Lord of glory. But He answered His disciples, who were anxiously inquiring about their glorification, according to the form of a slave: "To sit at my right hand or at my left, is not mine to give you, but to those for whom it has been prepared by my Father."

We have already stated He glorifies His own as God, and certainly as the Lord of glory, and still the Lord of glory was crucified, because God is rightly said to be crucified, not through the power of the divinity but through the weakness of the flesh. In the same way we say that He judges as God, that is, by His divine, not by His human power, and the Man Himself is going to judge, as the Lord of glory was crucified, for He says this clearly in the following words: "When the Son of Man shall come in his majesty, and all the angels with him, then all the nations will be gathered before him," and the other things which are made known in that passage of Scripture.

For, since both the good and the wicked are to see the judge of the living and the dead, the wicked will no doubt be unable to see Him except according to that form by which He is the Son of Man, but still in the glory in which He will judge. Moreover, the godless will undoubtedly not see the form of God in which He is equal to the Father, for they are not clean of heart, since "Blessed are the clean of heart for they shall see God."

And the vision itself is "face to face," which is promised to the just as their supreme reward, and this will come to pass when He shall deliver the Kingdom of God to the Father. There, He wants it understood, will also be the vision of His own form, when the whole of creation together with that form in which the Son of God has been made the Son of Man, has been made subject to God. Because, according to this form: "The Son Himself will be made subject to Him, who subjected all things to Him, that God may be all in all."

But that vision of the Son of Man, which has been prophesied, when all the nations will be gathered before Him, and they will say to Him: "Lord, when did we see thee hungry, thirsty, naked. . ." will neither be good for the wicked who will be sent into everlasting fire, nor the supreme good for the just. For He still has to call them to the kingdom which was prepared for them from the beginning of the world. He will say to these: "Come, blessed of my Father, into the Kingdom which was prepared for you," and so bring them to everlasting life.

But what is everlasting life if not "that they may know thee, the only true God and Him whom thou hast sent, Jesus Christ"? But then He will be in the glory of which He says to the Father: "that I had with thee before the world was made." Then He will deliver the kingdom to God and the Father, that the good servant may enter into the joy of his Lord. For the just man need never fear the judgment when he is shielded in the tabernacle, that is, active in the true faith of the Catholic Church.

LIVING VOICES-

A POSTSCRIPT

The Church has never lacked for men who proclaim, in word or in work, the marvels of God and His Christ. We have seen in our generation two such men in Pope John XXIII and President John Fitzgerald Kennedy. Part of their glory is that they are links in a living tradition through which the work of Jesus Christ continues through time.

"God created us without our cooperation; He will not save us without it." And so, God chooses to embrace certain "vessels of election" to cooperate in the work of bringing salvation to each generation. The teaching work that began so gloriously with St. Paul's mission has been continued through the ages by the constant stream of great Christian writers and preachers.

In this little volume there has been a glimpse of the treasures offered in THE FATHERS OF THE CHURCH *series, which, when completed, will make the voices of the Fathers available to all English-speaking people. This book, itself, is both a sample and an invitation, centering around the theme universally accepted and taught by all Catholics, that Christ is God, that Jesus is Lord.*

MEET

THE AUTHORS

ST. AMBROSE (pp. 21, 114, 154, 202, 205, 208, 258)

340-397. First a lawyer, then a governor, Ambrose was named Bishop of Milan while still a catechumen. He was instrumental in the conversion of St. Augustine. His feast is Dec. 7.

ST. AUGUSTINE (pp. 29, 39, 138, 222, 231, 245, 254, 264)

354-430. The famous Bishop of Hippo was the son of the illustrious St. Monica. He wrote extensively on theological, philosophical and ascetical subjects and was vigorous in his defense of the doctrine of the divinity of Christ. His feast is Aug. 28.

ST. BASIL (pp. 94, 119, 134, 158, 161, 184)

329-379. Another fearless defender of the divinity of Our Lord, Basil was an outstanding defender of the teachings of the Catholic Church in the Arian controversy. He ranks with St. Benedict as a founder of monasticism. His feast is June 14.

ST. BERNARD OF CLAIRVAUX (pp. 74, 103)

1090-1153. Considered by many as "The last of the Fathers," Bernard's most well-known works investigate the dignity of Mary, the Mother of God. However, his writings about our Lord are among the most inspirational and devotional in patrology. His feast is Aug. 20.

ST. CAESARIUS OF ARLES (p. 172)

470-543. Born in Burgundy and trained in a monastery at Lerins, Caesarius became Bishop of Arles in 503. The writings that he left during his long episcopate show that he drew heavily on the works of St. Ambrose and St. Augustine. His feast is Aug. 27.

CLEMENT OF ALEXANDRIA (p. 108)

150-215. Clement of Alexandria was one of the first Christian humanists. His learned works show that he used the famous libraries of ancient Alexandria extensively.

ST. CLEMENT OF ROME (pp. 188, 242)

1st century. Pope St. Clement I was the third successor of St. Peter and a contemporary of Sts. Peter and Paul. His feast is Nov. 23.

ST. CYPRIAN (pp. 124, 177)

200-258. A native of Africa, Cyprian became the leader of the Church in Africa through his learning and personality. His feast is Sept. 16.

EUSEBIUS (pp. 43, 81)

260-340. Bishop Eusebius of Caesaria took a leading part in the Council of Nicaea. He had studied in the famous library of Pamphilius and this may account for his tremendous interest in Church history.

ST. GREGORY THE GREAT (p. 250)

c540-604. Pope St. Gregory I was called to lead the Church through the chaotic conditions of the sixth century. His feast is Mar. 12.

ST. HILARY OF POITIERS (p. 215)

c300-368. From the brilliant mind of St. Hilary many learned treatises came explaining the nature of God. His feast is Jan. 14.

ST. IGNATIUS OF ANTIOCH (p. 85)

1st century. The valuable and beautiful letters of St. Ignatius teach precious lessons about the faith and ecclesiastical structure of the primitive Church. His feast is Feb. 1.

ST. JOHN CHRYSOSTOM (pp. 25, 180, 195)

347-407. Another in the great line of the Patriarchs of Constantinople, John Chrysostom was considered the finest preacher of his time. His feast is Jan. 27.

ST. JOHN DAMASCENE (pp. 68, 97)

690-749. John the Damascene is sometimes called "the last of the Greek Fathers." His great theological treatises are often used in the liturgy. His feast is Mar. 27.

ST. JUSTIN, MARTYR (pp. 50, 63)

c100-165. The layman, Justin, stands as the first of a long line of famous lay Christian apologists. His feast is Apr. 14.

ST. LEO THE GREAT (pp. 33, 53, 88)

c400-461. Surrounded by political and theological quarrels, Pope St. Leo I was a strong Pope during whose long reign the faith grew and prospered. His feast is Apr. 11.

ST. NICETA OF REMESIANA (p. 145)

c335-415. A devoted friend of St. Paulinus, St. Niceta was a missionary bishop in the present-day territory of Jugoslavia. His feast is June 22.

ST. PETER CHRYSOLOGUS (pp. 59, 236)

c400-450. This famous Archbishop of Ravenna was considered the equal of St. John Chrysostom in preaching ability. His feast is Dec. 4.

PRUDENTIUS (pp. 77, 149, 226)

348-424. Aurelus Prudentius Clemens was a citizen of Roman culture and rank. He was born in Spain, and held important political posts in the Empire. He had a fine grasp of Christian and pagan writers.

TERTULLIAN (pp. 168, 211)

2nd century. A well-educated convert who had a stormy theological career. He is well known for the idea that the blood of martyrs is the seed of Christians.

ST. VALERIAN (p. 129)

5th century. St. Valerian worked in Southern France and is noted for his intense loyalty to the Holy See. His feast is kept in some places on July 23.

WITNESS

OF THE AGES

	99	St.	Clement of Rome
	107	St.	Ignatius of Antioch
100 —	165	St.	Justin Martyr
150 —	215		Clement of Alexandria
150 —	220		Tertullian
200 —	258	St.	Cyprian
260 —	340		Eusebius of Caesarea
300 —	368	St.	Hilary of Poitiers
329 —	379	St.	Basil
335 —	415	St.	Niceta of Remesiana
340 —	397	St.	Ambrose
347 —	407	St.	John Chrysostom
348 —	424		Prudentius
354 —	430	St.	Augustine
400 —	461	St.	Leo the Great
400 —	450	St.	Peter Chrysologus
450 —	500	St.	Valerian
470 —	543	St.	Caesarius of Arles
540 —	604	St.	Gregory the Great
690 —	749	St.	John Damascene
1090 —	1153	St.	Bernard of Clairvaux

INDEX

Abraham	103, 156, 157
Adam	94-95, 125, 149, 196, 224, 237
Alberione, Fr.	152
Ambrose, St.	21, 114, 154, 202, 205, 208, 258, 273
Amos	260
Angels	22, 32, 51, 59-62, 64, 104, 120, 145, 155, 190, 238
Ascension	84, 232-234, 254
Augustine, St.	29, 39, 138, 222, 231, 245, 254, 264, 273
Baptism	101, 105, 125, 147, 153, 154-156, 158, 161-167, 178, 209, 223, 245-247, 255
Basil, St.	94, 119, 134, 158, 161, 184, 273
Bernard, St.	74, 103, 273
Bethlehem	49, 51-52, 64-66
Birth of Christ	33-36, 64-65, 77-78, 120, 216, 255
Bridegroom	41, 74
Caesarius, St.	172, 273
Catholic	41, 92, 271
Christ	20, 21, 33, 44-45, 53, 72-73, 81, 86, 96, 102, 109, 116, 119, 121, 131, 133-134, 161-162, 173-174, 190, 211, 214, 222-225, 227, 232, 234, 251, see also, Jesus.
Christians	67, 81, 88, 276
Christmas	49, 107
Circumcision	103-105, 164-165, 208-210
Clement of Alexandria	108, 274
Clement, St.	188, 242, 274
Crucifixion	37-38, 71, 80, 90, 104, 128, 173,

	186, 194, 195-198, 205-207, 213, 227, 248-249, 268
Cyprian, St.	124, 177, 274
Cyril of Alexandria, St.	102
David, King	44-46, 53, 66-67, 86, 106, 184
Death	29-30, 41, 56, 61, 79, 86, 89, 94, 125, 186, 213, 218, 222, 227, 230, 238, 265
Devils	30-31, 94, 118, 169, 198, 265
Easter	107, 229
Egypt	65, 228
Elias	117
Emmanuel	chap. 2, p. 48 ff.
Eunuch	246-247
Eusebius of Caesarea	43, 81, 274
Eve	60
Faith	28, 30, 41, 74, 129, 171, 178
Father, The	15, 26-27, 36-38, 47, 48, 53, 57, 66-67, 68-69, 72, 77, 81-84, 92, 97-102, 105, 109-110, 119-121, 124-125, 135, 145, 162, 169, 173, 177, 179, 215-221, 225, 254, 260, 264
Form of God,...of a slave	32, 265-267
Gabriel	59-61, 104
Gregory, St.	250, 275
Hebrews	44, 46, 226
Herod	26, 64-65
High Priest	44-46, 66, 89, 122, 147, 149, 188, 226
Hilary, St.	215, 275
Holy Redeemer	94
Holy Spirit	15, 21, 26, 33, 45, 51, 64, 68-69, 72, 74, 81, 101, 139, 156, 161, 170, 177-179, 220, 255, 264
Holy Trinity	19, 32, 48, 130, 154-156, 179, 255
Horn	160

Humanity of Christ	34, 41, 70, 79-80, 146, 220, 264, 266, see also Incarnation, birth.
Hypostatic Union	69-71, 80, 99
Ignatius of Antioch, St.	85, 275
Incarnation	25-28, 49, 54, 70, 80, 88, 96, 97, 99, 104, 156, 187, 216
Isaac	196
Isaias	45, 48, 50-51, 63, 66, 193
Jacob	50, 66, 187, 227
Jeremias	65
Jerusalem	52, 202
Jesse	50
Jesus	15, 33-34, 43, 51, 75-76, 85, 102, 103, 109-110, 115, 145, 162, 176, 188-192, 215-217, 222, 242, 253, 258, 262-263. See also Christ.
Jews	50, 195, 212
John, St.	19-20, 21-23, 25, 53, 199-201, 202-203, 229
John Chrysostom, St.	25, 180, 195, 275
John Damascene, St.	68, 97, 275
John the Baptist, St.	37, 92, 125, 156
John XXIII, Pope	151, 271
Joseph, St.	59-60, 64-65, 104, 120, 181
Juda	50, 51, 64
Judas	181-182
Justin, Martyr, St.	50, 63, 275
Kennedy, John F.	271
Lazarus	79, 114-116, 150, 257
Leo, St.	33, 53, 70, 88, 275
Luke, St.	25, 59, 79, 104, 152
Magi	37, 63-65, 92, 131, 227
Manger	103, 120, 131
Mark, St.	25
Marmion, Abbot Columba	49
Mary, the Blessed Virgin	24, 33-36, 40, 48, 50-51, 56-58, 59-62, 63-65, 68-69, 72, 77-78, 80, 85, 87, 88, 92-93, 94-95, 103, 150, 155-157, 199-200, 202-204,

	205, 211, 217, 237, 255, 265
Mary Magdalen, St.	236-237
Mass	252-253
Matthew, St.	25
Mediator	29-32, 33, 39, 54, 77, 88, 103, 222, 224-225
Melchisedech	66, 156
Micheas	51
Moses	43, 66, 108, 226, 262-263
Mystical Body	153, 257
Naaman	154
Nazareth	64, 75
Niceta of Remesiana, St.	145, 276
Only-begotten Son	38, 54, 147, 159, 164
Passion	118, 126, 151, 173, 186, 188, 193, 205-207, 218, 255
Paul, St.	15, 53, 74, 88-89, 129, 156, 173, 178, 184, 185, 186, 194, 221, 222, 224, 230, 248, 250-251, 258, 262, 271
Paul VI, Pope	20
Peace	136-137, 140-141, 147, 162
Pentecost	107, 152
Peter, St.	38, 75, 92, 117, 153, 168, 173, 177, 180-181, 245, 258, 262
Peter, Chrysologus, St.	59, 236, 276
Philip, deacon	246-247
Pontius Pilate	87, 195-198
Prophets	44-45, 62, 108, 121, 169, 213
Precious Blood	66, 86, 89, 135, 137, 194, 208
Prudentius	77, 149, 226, 276
Quirinius	52, 64
Rachel	65
Resurrection	31, 84, 86, 97, 114, 117, 148, 151, 177, 194, 213, 229, 231-235, 236-240, 246-247, 262
Savior	43, 100, 104-105, 112, 131, 145, 188, 226
Sermon on the Mount	138-144
Solomon	121

Son of God   23, 37-38, 51, 54, 68, 80, 82,
                          165, 181, 211, 217, 220, 263
Son of Man   37-38, 71, 79-80, 146, 220, 264,
                          270
Stephen, St.   221, 262
Tertullian   168, 211, 276
Tiberius Caesar   25
Unicorn   160
Valerian, St.   129, 276
Valentinus   95
Vatican II   20
Word, The   19, 21-23, 26-28, 31, 33, 36, 46,
                          48, 53, 57-58, 68-70, 77, 80,
                          82-83, 88, 92-93, 99, 109, 112,
                          128, 187
Zacharias   98